1

How to Engage, Connect, & Captivate:

Become the Social Presence You've Always Wanted To Be. Small Talk, Meaningful Communication, & Deep Connections

By Patrick King
Social Interaction and
Conversation Coach at
www.PatrickKingConsulting
.com

Table of Contents

CHAPTER 1. CONVERSATIONAL LANDMINES　　7

WHAT TO AVOID 1: PLAYING AT BEING THE COOL GUY 8
WHAT TO AVOID 2: BEING A BORING KNOW-IT-ALL　14
WHAT TO AVOID 3: BRINGING YOUR EGO TO THE PARTY

20
THING TO AVOID 4: BRAGGING　　27
THING TO AVOID 5: MISMATCHED ENERGY　　33

CHAPTER 2. GET YOURSELF RIGHT　　39

READING OUT LOUD　　50
CHOOSE A ROLE MODEL　　58
LIFE IS A SERIES OF STORIES　　67
PLUMPING UP YOUR CONVERSATION RESUME　　75

CHAPTER 3. SET THE MOOD　　85

DIVULGING　　85
SHARING MORE　　86
NO JUDGING　　95
SELF-ENTERTAINING AND AMUSEMENT　　105

**CHAPTER 4. INTERACT AND PARTICIPATE
FULLY**　　117

QUESTIONS – AN UNDERRATED SUPERPOWER　　117
THE SOCRATIC METHOD　　121
THE CONVERSATIONAL NARCISSISM RATIO　　127
WHAT WOULD CONAN DO AND CURIOSITY　　138

CHAPTER 5. ENGAGEMENT　　153

VALIDATION **154**

STEP 1 – HOW TO BE PRESENT: LISTEN! 155

STEP 2 – HOW TO REFLECT: ASK QUESTIONS 158

STEP 3 – HOW TO MINDREAD: USE FEELING WORDS 162

STEP 4 – HOW TO FIND CONTEXT: VALIDATE AND CENTER THEIR EXPERIENCE 165

STEP 5 – HOW TO NORMALIZE: REFRAIN FROM JUDGMENT

168

STEP 6 – HOW TO SHOW GENUINE VALIDATION: BE REAL

173

HPM **176**

SBR **183**

YOUR PATTERNS **190**

THE SEARCH FOR SIMILARITY AND FAMILIARITY **191**

CHAPTER 6: LIGHT SPEED **203**

HUMOR AND MISDIRECTION **203**

THE POWER OF IMPROV **219**

DON'T HOLD ON TOO TIGHTLY 222

LEARN TO MAKE QUICK CONNECTIONS 227

HAVE A LITTLE FAITH 234

THE 1:1:1 METHOD OF STORYTELLING **236**

CONVERSATIONAL DIVERSITY **248**

HYPOTHETICALS 248

THINK OUT LOUD 252

SUMMARY GUIDE **257**

Chapter 1. Conversational Landmines

Are you one of those people who "hates small talk"?

When you think about it, what you might really hate is *being bad* at small talk. Learning how to chit chat casually with people you're not very familiar with can seem difficult or boring—if you don't know what you're doing. Yes, many people out there seem to be blessed with the social butterfly gene that allows them to easily slip into charming conversation with just about anyone, but if you're not one of those people, don't worry: you can learn.

Becoming good at conversation is not something we usually think of as a skill to practice and master, but fortunately just a little effort can make you far more confident, more approachable, and a much better listener!

In this book we'll be looking at how to prepare to be a good conversationalist even before you open your mouth, how to get in the right frame of mind, how to engage meaningfully with others, as well as all the unspoken rules that make the difference between a dead-end conversation and you charming the socks off a person you met just two minutes ago.

Before we dive in, however, let's take a closer look at what *not* to do. You don't want a conversation to fizzle into awkward silence, but you also don't want to try so hard that you make other people uncomfortable. Improving your conversation skills is not about being phony, manipulative or desperate—the opposite, in fact!

What to Avoid 1: Playing at Being the Cool Guy

We all know what it looks like to be "good with people." To be confident, relaxed, charming and witty. To tell good stories and give compliments that have people eating out of the palm of your hand . . . in other words, to be that *cool guy*.

But can you picture it, right now? You're at a social gathering and there's that one awkward guy, clearly nervous, maybe overdressed, who might as well be wearing a sign over his head saying, "I read a book about how to look cool and confident." You know how it goes. You try to talk to such a person, and you get the distinct impression that what they say has been rehearsed in a mirror beforehand. He's talking too loud, he seems uncomfortable and pushy. It's simple: it's all fake.

A lot of us, particularly if we're quite or introverted people, mistakenly believe that being more sociable and engaging in conversation means changing who we are as people. We may have an image of who that popular, cool person is and think that, if we want to succeed socially, we need to mimic that.

But mimicry is actually the worst thing you can do. Because trying to be someone who you're not will never, ever work. The best you can do is be a subpar copy of someone else. This would be okay except for the fact that people are a lot smarter than they may seem, and can almost always tell that you're not being authentic. So, instead of connecting genuinely to people and closing that gap between you, you only put up further barriers, and possibly create more tension.

Calling this mistake the "cool guy" doesn't mean it only applies to men, or to people who want to come across as ultra-confident. It refers to any person who is actively and transparently seeking to portray themselves in a particular way. In other words, it's trying to be someone else. Your version of the "cool guy" might be to pretend you like what the group likes, or dress in a way that is uncomfortable but you feel helps you fit in. Maybe you try too hard to appear friendly and easy going that your smile eventually becomes forced, and people notice the opposite of what you intend—that you actually seem stressed out.

One way that socializing can become inauthentic is through alcohol. Many people genuinely think that they *need* to drink, since they see their sober selves as inadequate, and being a little drunk makes it easier to play some other role, to be someone else. Another example is rehearsed jokes or pickup lines—all likely to be experienced as insincere and outright fake. What people will see is not the mask, but the effort you've made to put on that mask.

Of course, being inauthentic doesn't have to be anything dramatic. If you simply hold the mindset that you don't quite like yourself, and wish you were someone different, you cannot help but unconsciously communicating this to others. Someone who engages with others while holding the belief "I need to be XYZ" will behave very differently from someone who is merely attempting to connect with others, to learn about them, and to share who they are.

It may seem strange to start a book like this with a word on authenticity—isn't it a contradiction to read a book about how to be different, that tells you not to try too hard to be something you're not? But this is a subtle and important point: *we do not have to change who we are* to be better communicators and more skilful at conversation. But we can become better at expressing what we are to others.

The goal is not to build up a false front, an alter ego that is good at small talk. Rather, the goal is to become better at letting people see who you are, as you are, and doing the same for them. If you can connect authentically to others in this way, you will be perceived as charismatic, interesting and likeable. But if you are noticeably *trying* to be all these things, people cannot help but perceive the trying!

How can you avoid the trap of trying to be your own version of the "cool guy"?

Firstly, keep reminding yourself that being a great conversationalist is not about rehearsing, saying this or that, or acting. It's not about being a perfect and invulnerable person. Think about who you are, and what distinguishes you from everyone else. The people that love you—what do they see in you? That essence that makes you who you are—there's no need to hide it!

Consider an example. In a conversation, someone is clearly nervous and uncomfortable, but they're trying vehemently to hide the fact. They talk loudly and force a laugh, even acting a little cocky. What is your response to them? Now think about someone else, who is also clearly nervous and uncomfortable. But imagine that this person smiles simply at you, shrugs and says, "I'm going to be honest with you, I'm pretty nervous right now!" How is your reaction to them different?

Being introverted, softly spoken or quiet doesn't mean that you cannot connect with others. Turn up meaningfully in conversations, as you are and with genuineness, and you engage with others far quicker than if you were merely pretending otherwise. In this rest of this book, if you read a suggestion or technique and it really doesn't feel right to you, then simply don't use it! Authenticity is more important.

- As you talk to people, try to recall a compliment you've received in the past that made you feel like a million dollars. Smile and relax in the knowledge that you, just as you are, are awesome!
- Don't rush when you talk. You don't have to quickly share everything

interesting about yourself in one go. Just be curious about where the conversational flow is going.

- Don't be afraid to say something a little unexpected. When you follow a safe formula, you're boring. Why not highlight the most unusual parts of your personality instead?
- Similarly, don't be afraid to admit you don't know something, have made a mistake, or don't understand. A confident confession is more endearing than someone fumbling to pretend they're on top of things when they aren't.

What to Avoid 2: Being a Boring Know-It-All

The previous mistake is all about assuming that we have to be someone else, to be cool and confident, if we want to be good conversationalists. This mistake is similar, in that we imagine that we have to be super smart, logical, and *right* in order for others to like us and want to talk to us.

Picture two acquaintances chatting, and one person says, "I love George Eliot! He was one of my favorite authors growing up!" The other person's ears prick and they jump in and immediately say, "George Eliot? You know that's a woman, right? George Eliot is just her pen name." The first person then says, "Oh? Really? So *Vanity Fair* was written by a woman?" The rest of the conversation veers off as the other person smugly informs them that no, *Vanity Fair* was in actual fact written by William Makepeace Thackery, who was, obviously, a man . . .

In no time, the conversation becomes the one person haughtily giving the other a lesson on Victorian Literature, as the eyes of the first quietly glaze over in boredom. What's gone wrong here?

Let's be honest: it's human nature to want to be right. Most of us like to feel that we're smart or in-the-know, and can't help but leap in to fix a correction or share our knowledge and skill with others. But the problem is obvious—people don't have conversations with each other merely to gather new data. If you get carried away being super logical and pedantic, you miss the real point of human conversation, which is to connect emotionally.

What is important is to sustain a pleasant, lively flow of banter that brings both people closer together. If you keep getting distracted by the veracity of little details (or worse, keeping of who is right and who is wrong), then you are killing that conversational flow dead in its tracks. If we're honest, most of us engage in this pedantic behavior not because we're sticklers for accuracy or champions for The Truth but merely because we want to show off!

Picture someone who won't let something go, even when the conversation has moved on. Or imagine someone who makes a point of letting everyone else know how wrong they are, while they proceed to correct and enlighten them. Not much fun, right? Being overly logical means you are inflexible, rigid and lacking in the ability to think outside the box or have a little humor. In other words, you're boring company.

But let's dig deeper—why do people fall into this trap? For some people, being the clever know-it-all is one form of inauthenticity, as discussed in the previous section. Being a smarty pants can feel like a useful shield, or an intimidating mask or persona to hide behind in the hopes that other people will be impressed or convinced that we're likeable or valuable. For some people, emphasizing their own intellect speaks to an insecurity in this area, and conversations for them become something like battle grounds, rather than opportunities to connect and have fun with others.

Think about how the conversational tone might have been different if the person in the example simply said, "I think George Eliot is actually a woman? If I was giving myself a male pseudonym, I'd go with something more exciting that *George* though, wouldn't you?" Or imagine if the person had simply let the mistake slide. Does it really matter, ultimately, if someone is mistaken?

This is something important to understand when we think about connecting with others. The content of a conversation is not all that important, but the *way* that content is conveyed makes all the difference. To put it differently, a conversation is primarily a flow of energy and feeling, rather than an exchange of information. If you can connect to someone on a personal, emotional level, it is entirely irrelevant what specific details you talk about to get there.

So, if someone says, "I wonder if ancient Aramaic had swear words?" you could cut the conversation short to Google it on your phone, or follow it up with a response that keeps the conversation flowing instead: "Ha, can you imagine? Jesus swearing at his carpentry would make a pretty funny sketch." If someone pronounces something wrong, simply pronounce it accurately yourself, and avoid pompously saying, "*Well, actually . . .*"

It's all about shifting your perspective and understanding what your real goal is in having a conversation in the first place. You don't have to prove yourself to anyone, impress them or demonstrate your intelligence. You certainly don't have to put anyone else down. Rather, a conversation is about people and the connection they make, not the facts they share.

Consider the statement, "Oh, I would so love to run away and live in Chile for a year. People there live in such poverty, and I'd love to make a difference in a small way." You could respond to the purely factual data in the statement and pipe in by saying that Chile actually has lower poverty rates than the US. Or, you could respond to the *emotional content* of what's been shared with you, and notice how excited the person is by the prospect of doing good in the world.

The first response will be technically correct, but it's the second that will keep the dialogue going, and foster a meaningful connection with the other person. If you ever are tempted to be a know-it-all in conversations, try to put yourself in the other person's shoes. Do *you* like people more just because they always have the right answer? Do you feel strongly connected to people just after they butt into the conversation to tell you you're wrong? Chances are, what you are drawn to is someone who is listening, empathetic, easy going, kind and receptive. Who is "right" is almost irrelevant!

- Often, we are quick to assume that people are wrong, when what's really happened is that we just don't quite understand their viewpoint. Instead of writing off their opinion, ask them more about it. You might be surprised at what you learn.

- Treat other people as the experts. Ask them to talk about something *they* understand deeply. Then listen.
- Have an attitude of wonder and curiosity, and keep things open ended. Your goal is not to resolve a question, but to keep up the flow of an enjoyable discussion about what it could be.
- Use humor. Be playful and creative. *Knowing* something is boring—isn't it more fun to imagine possibilities, or think about what you don't yet understand?

What to Avoid 3: Bringing Your Ego to the Party

Closely connected to the above is the person that's not only always right about facts and data, but also seems to insist that their tastes and opinions are the right ones, too. This is the person who will gleefully play "thought police" in a group of people, act like a snob, or quietly (or not so quietly) judge others for their beliefs and actions.

This is the stubborn person who "tells it like it is" and flat-out refuses to entertain anybody's perspective but their own, i.e., the best one.

There isn't enough space in this small book to cover all the vast and colorful ways that the ego can make its presence known, but suffice to say that this conversational mistake is one where we forget that it takes *two* to tango. Again, it comes down to fundamental beliefs about what conversations are actually for. If you are desperately playing the cool guy, you might think, "Conversations are ways to convince people to like me and accept me." If you are a know-it-all, you may think conversations are ways to prove your superior intellect and show off.

For some people, though, conversations can be like wrestling matches where you have to beat down your opponents. They imagine themselves on soap boxes, preaching their own opinion and trying to make everyone else see that it's the right one. When the ego is in charge, conversations are a platform not for connection, but for combat. Alternatively, a dialogue isn't even felt to be a dialogue at all, but rather a captive audience who are compelled to watch your performance as you entertain or inform or chastise. The flow doesn't go both ways—the audience is at most expected to applaud at the right moments.

Though we've all known people who dramatically dominate conversations this way, the truth is that any one of us can become self-centered in conversation, even if we see ourselves as shy and retiring. For example, you may nervously chatter on about something without pausing and, since you're constantly planning what you'll say next, you never really hear what the other person is saying. In other words, having low confidence and fretting about how we appear can often be the thing that makes us most selfish in conversation!

When you bring your ego to the party, your goal again shifts away from connecting with others, and onto supporting and bolstering your own ego. This hinders your ability to listen to and empathize with other people (because, well, you're the most important person in the conversation), and it definitely prevents you from learning anything new (what's there to learn when you already know everything?).

Conversations are not contests, where there can only be one victor, the one who can argue their case best. Though it's always important to be honest and true to yourself, the reality is that it's seldom appropriate or worthwhile getting into heated "debates" where you try to one up the other person. Not only will you *not* change their mind, but you'll also lose any possible connection.

Good conversations flow. They're dynamic and flexible, with energy moving freely between both people. If you hog all the time to make a speech about something, you stop the flow. If you keep insisting on your opinion, you similarly strangle that back-and-forth. Either people will push back and you'll have an argument, or they'll detach and likely avoid you in future. Talking to abrasive, all-or-nothing types can be draining!

Instead, remind yourself that *any* two people can have a good conversation, and they don't need to agree to do so. The point of the conversation is not to reach consensus, but to enjoy sharing opinions, potentially even learning from one another. The antidote to a big fat ego in conversation is curiosity. Forget about yourself for a while and try to enter into the world of the other person, with respect and curiosity. You already know all about your perspective and opinions, so why rehash them? It's far more exciting to learn about all those opinions you *don't* have.

Practice the art of respectful disagreement. Notice how you can completely disagree with someone without losing the connection between you. Use a little humor, ask thoughtful questions, or shift the topic to something that you do both agree on. Our ego tells us that everything like us is good and everything unlike us is bad, but is that really true? Can't we accept difference in others—or even celebrate it?

Take a look at the following examples, and see if you can spot the difference in perspective, i.e. how the person sees the main goals of conversation.

"Have you watched The Queen's Gambit?"

"Uh . . . you mean that thing on Netflix? Honestly, I got bored after the first episode."

"Really? I totally got sucked in. I'm almost considering learning chess . . ."

"You can't be serious. That's not *at all* what playing chess is like, you know."

"Sure. It's just a bit of escapism, I guess . . ." (They say, thinking about their own escape from the conversation.)

"That's the problem right there. Escapism. *I* personally can't stand the junk they're churning out these days. I mean, read a book, right?"

"Uh, I guess . . ."

"So, who's your favorite Victorian author?"

"Huh?"

"Mine's George Eliot. A lot of people can't appreciate that kind of thing—attention span's too short! But I do. I sometimes think I could have been George Eliot in a past life! People don't appreciate literature anymore, it's criminal. Too easy to sit in front of the TV and binge watch the garbage they make these days . . . of course, I don't even own a TV. Do *you* own a TV? I read this study the other day about the effects of TV on . . ."

And so on. In a way, this person has "won" the conversation. They are king of castle, and the other person likely feels bad. But as far as creating connection and warmth, or enjoying a lively conversation, it's a solid one out of ten. Consider instead:

"Have you watched The Queen's Gambit?"

"Uh . . . you mean that thing on Netflix? Honestly, I got bored after the first episode."

"Really? I totally got sucked in. I'm almost considering learning chess . . ."

"Yeah, I bet! I have to be honest, chess bores me to tears. But the clothes in that show? I can get behind that!"

"Exactly! They make being a chess prodigy look so elegant."

"And here's me sitting in my Hello Kitty sweatpants . . ."

"Don't even get me started! Are you working from home, then . . .?"

Notice that in both conversations, there is disagreement. But in the second, this disagreement is seamlessly skipped over to land on something else that can keep the conversation flowing, whereas in the first, the conversation sputters and stalls on the person's insistence on lecturing the other and giving them a lesson about good taste—i.e., snobbery! Ego shuts conversations down, whereas curiosity, humor and empathy keep them alive and flowing.

- Tell yourself that the person in front of you has something amazing to teach you or share with you. Approach the conversation as a way to find out what that is.
- It may seem too simple, but a good trick is to act as though you already know this person thinks you're great. This will put you at ease and curb the desire to puff up your ego—you don't have anything to prove!
- See conversations as a tennis match, and don't forget to volley back the "ball" after you've spoken for a while. Keep asking them questions, rather than looking for a way to butt in with your observations.
- Remember the saying: people will usually forget what you say, but they will never forget how you made them feel!

Thing to Avoid 4: Bragging

It's perfectly natural to want others to think positively of you. It's human nature to want to be liked, respected, even admired. And in dating, it's all part of the game to hope that the people you're into are also into you. However, we can end up shooting ourselves in the foot if we are too direct about promoting ourselves, in other words, if we are seen to be bragging.

You might sincerely think you are awesome, or you may have a low self-esteem and are compensating with an over-the-top act of confidence. Either way, bragging has the opposite effect of what we'd really like it to; people may be unimpressed and find you arrogant, even to the extent where they think worse of you than if you'd said nothing at all.

It's one of the unspoken rules of human socialization: you are not meant to blow your own trumpet! Even if you do happen to be beautiful, accomplished, intelligent or super interesting, there's something about boldly claiming the fact that diminishes it in other people's eyes. Far better to merely be who you are, carry yourself with quiet assurance, and let other people recognize how awesome you are.

Now, before you assume that this conversational mistake doesn't apply to you, think twice, and be honest about whether you may have indulged in a little "humblebragging" here and there. We've all seen it happen, and we all respond to it in similar ways, either finding it amusing at best or annoying at worst. The humblebrag is a transparent attempt to talk about how amazing you are while at the same time not appearing to be. It's almost worse than bragging, since the person likely realizes that bragging isn't appropriate . . . but wants to do it anyway, and maybe even be praised for it.

"Ugh, I hate my hair. It's so long and thick it takes me *ages* to brush. Yesterday this complete stranger said it was beautiful—so embarrassing!"

"I just want to say that yes, I've donated over one hundred thousand dollars to this cause, but please, I only wish I could do more. I'm just so grateful that I've had the seemingly unlimited financial success to make a difference, no matter how small . . ."

"Phew! Just come back from Bali. I am *exhausted*. The flight was delayed by a half hour but thank God my PA and financial advisor were there to keep me sane. So blessed! If she wasn't keeping an eye on me who knows how big my Gucci addiction would be . . ."

These humblebrags are obviously quite . . . obvious. And that's just the problem: they're usually not subtle (after all, you don't want the other person to mistakenly think you're actually humble) and make the other person feel that you are more concerned with flattering yourself than having a genuine connection with them. It's yet another barrier to genuine, enjoyable conversation.

The ironic thing about being boastful or using false modesty is that it usually comes from its opposite—from insecurity, or the belief that we need to be perfectly amazing before we are worth talking to or liking. A better tactic by far is to actually embrace your imperfections. Confidently own up to all your flaws and quirks and, counterintuitively, you immediately seem more charming and real to people.

The presence of someone who is perfect (or trying to be!) can put everyone else on edge.

It's far more comfortable to talk to someone who is honest, normal, and genuinely humble. In fact, if impressing others is your goal, the best way to do it is to simply be an impressive person, and then *downplay* your achievements. There's a reason self-deprecating people are so likeable. They seem to communicate a quiet, easy confidence in themselves, no need for approval from others, and a good sense of humor to boot. All very attractive qualities to have!

At the very least, if you really are feeling proud of yourself or want to brag a little about something, do it in a way where you have some plausible deniability. People don't like others who are trying too hard to be who they aren't, or portray themselves in an overly flattering light. If you do boast and are called out on it, you can save the situation by being candid and owning up to it—after all, we've all done it!

Here are some ways to be genuinely humble and unpretentious:

- Laugh at yourself—you'll put other people at ease and show that you're not primarily concerned with boosting your own ego.

- Generally, avoid talking about your accomplishments at all, since it can be a fine line between bragging and just stating—rather, let your achievements speak for themselves, if you really must.

- Focus on the other person and make them feel good. Play up their virtues with compliments and ask plenty of questions to show where your real interest lies—in the other person.

- Be a little self-deprecating—it can be so refreshing when people are aware of their own flaws. This self-awareness can make you seem more human, more relatable, and even more lovable. People may feel that you're more likely to be compassionate to *them* if you happily accept who *you* are.

- Ask for people's opinions and be interested in what they tell you. If you disagree, treat this disagreement as just another interesting part of the conversation!

Thing to Avoid 5: Mismatched Energy

One scenario goes like this: someone is a bit annoyed and feeling down at a party, and a person who's trying to talk to them is a little tipsy and feeling chatty and happy. No matter what the first one says, the second seems to respond with jokes and encouragement to "cheer up!" The conversation fizzles for understandable reasons—these two are just not in the same place, emotionally.

However, if the second person noticed that the first was feeling a bit annoyed and down, they might dial things back a little and have a more quiet, relaxed chat instead. If the first person also noticed the other's energy, they may meet them halfway by pepping up a little. If they can both find their way toward a shared emotional frame, then a meaningful conversation is suddenly possible.

Though the previous four small talk mistakes may have seemed obvious, this last one is far more subtle. If good communication is about establishing that human connection with someone else, then you can think of mismatched energies as a barrier to that proper connection. You could say and do all the right things, but if your energy is weird or vastly different from the person you're talking to, it's unlikely you'll feel "on the same wavelength."

There's nothing woo woo or mystical about "energy." It refers not only to the enthusiasm and degree of excitement you have as you talk, but it's about the *kind* of energy you're holding. What some call passionate and bubbly others may perceive as pushy or even threatening. You may feel calm and content yet it may come across as boring.

So, how you do you become aware of and optimize your energy when doing small talk? A simple trick is to take your lead from the other person. If they're talking quietly, being low key about things and acting generally relaxed, follow suit and use the same tone and volume of voice, matching their gestures and posture. If they're eager and talking quickly, you can communicate that you are alongside them by doing the same.

It's not rocket science. If you want to show someone that you're happy to join them in a shared conversation, you'll foster feelings of bonding and good chemistry if you're both painting from the same palette, so to speak. You may do this naturally, but the next conversation you're in, pay attention and see if you can deliberately calibrate your energy top more closely match and support the other person's.

Avoid extreme low or extreme high energy states (nobody likes an over-the-top hyper person or else the human equivalent of Eeyore) and try to modulate and vary your emotional pitch to keep things interesting. If you notice yourself getting all serious, lighten it up again to keep your listener's interest and ensure the conversation doesn't stall or stagnate, or vice versa. If you can mirror your conversation partner's energy levels, you communicate to them on a very primal level that you are *with them*, feeling similarly, inhabiting the same emotional universe and, essentially, in agreement. This can feel very flattering for the other party—they may not even understand exactly why they feel so close and connected to you!

Here are some ways to mirror or match your energy to the other person:

- Make your tone of voice, as well as the volume, the same as theirs.
- Mimic their posture or body language. (Not too closely, though, you don't want to freak them out!)
- Reflect back a few noteworthy phrases or words they use.
- If it's appropriate, slightly shift your accent to more closely resemble theirs, or emphasize the points where your manner of speech is like theirs—you're not being fake, only enhancing the ways you're literally "speaking their language."
- Match their level of formality, for example don't be too casual if they're being formal.
- Notice the tone of what they're actually saying and reflect that back. If they're sharing a personal, humorous anecdote, for example, don't respond in a detached, academic way, or vice versa.

Ultimately, learning to be better at small talk is learning to be a better conversationalist, all round. And to do that we need to rethink how we understand the *goals* of any interaction with others. When we can frame conversation as a way to encounter others, to learn, to experience them and their viewpoints, to play, explore, or simply enjoy sharing, then we are halfway to becoming masters at small talk.

Takeaways

- Small talk is not a mysterious inbuilt trait but a skill anyone can learn and master. Being better at conversation is about understanding the real goal of any small talk: to foster closer and more genuine human connections with others.
- There are many barriers to this connection, and these are habits and mindsets to avoid. If we treat the goal of conversation as a way to play at being an ideal version of ourselves (the cool guy), we risk coming across as fake, desperate, or unlikable.
- If we see the goal of conversation as a chance to prove how right or how intelligent we are, we miss an opportunity to genuinely learn about the

other person and enjoy one of the main perks of dialogue: delving into someone else's perspective.

- If we see the goal of conversation as a battle or context to win, or a way to demonstrate our superiority, we treat our conversation partners like enemies or merely an audience, and this definitely stops the natural flow of conversation and prevents bonding.
- If we see the goal of conversation as a way to prove our value as human beings, we may be tempted to brag and boast. But this has the opposite effect and make us unlikable—plus, humble bragging is nearly always very transparent!
- Finally, a big barrier to genuine connection and rapport is simply not being on the same wavelength, or mismatched energies. We can learn to be better at this by matching our posture, what we're saying, and how we speak to the person we're talking to.

Chapter 2. Get Yourself Right

There's more to conversation than thinking off the cuff and creating witty banter out of nothing at all. Very few of us are capable of doing that on a consistent basis. What's far more sustainable, easy, and practical is *preparing* for a conversation beforehand. This means almost front-loading what you're going to say, which has two benefits—one, you're ready and able to respond in conversations, and two, you're probably more comfortable because you feel prepared.

But to be clear, you're not preparing for particular conversations like they are job interviews—rather, you are priming yourself to be able to shine in social exchanges in general. There's a distinct difference between the two. We've already seen that trying too hard to be the cool guy can have the opposite effect. Rather, being prepared is like turning up to an exercise class wearing trainers and sweatpants. You might not know exactly what exercise you'll be doing that day, but by being dressed appropriately, you're ready to respond more spontaneously to whatever happens. Good conversation is like that—you come prepared, but not necessarily with a script written in stone.

Don't worry about appearing forced or tackling the problem in a serious and overly formal way. Though it might seem counterintuitive, preparing well and making deliberate efforts to perform better in natural conversation can actually make you *more* spontaneous and relaxed. When you prepare for conversations, you'll find being witty much easier.

So, the first step to witty banter and small talk is to get ready psychologically—so you're not caught with your pants down in meeting someone new. What exactly does this mean? Think about when you just wake up and your voice is gravelly and incomprehensible. Your thoughts are unorganized and swirling, and anything that comes out of your mouth is likely to be responded to with a ". . . what did you say?"

When you're only half-awake, you're caught off guard when you have to respond to anything, and you have a lack of focus and awareness. This is our social status quo— how we normally move through and navigate the world. So, warming up mentally is about beginning to stretch and gingerly flex our social muscles so we're ready for action.

If you're out at a bar or networking event, you only have one shot at making the right impression. If you fall flat on your face, as will inevitably happen from time to time, guess what? That was your one shot at the goal—will you make the most of it?

Recall that as children, we were always admonished to never talk to strangers. This well-meaning instruction might have served us well in our childhood, when we were likely to be gullible prey to sly criminals. *Stranger danger* was a real thing to be avoided.

In public places, we plug our ears with headphones and glue our faces to our phones, preferring to keep our interactions with people we don't know to the bare minimum. But is this habit still serving us well? Likely not if our goal is to become better at conversation and charm. We should quickly let go of this tendency because, as adults, it only serves to keep us isolated from others. It locks us in a social prison of our own making, and it keeps us socially cold for occasions when we need to be *on*. At the very least, it leaves us woefully unprepared for engaging with people, exposed as if we were ambushed in the middle of the night.

A 2014 study by Epley and Schroeder divided commuters on trains and buses into three groups—the first was instructed to interact with a stranger near them, the second to keep to themselves, and the third to commute as normal. Even though participants in each group predicted feeling more positive if they kept to themselves, the outcome of the experiment was the opposite. At the end of their ride, the group of commuters who connected with a stranger reported a more positive experience than those who remained disconnected. It *seems* we believe that only awkwardness will ensue with a stranger, when instead an unexpected connection creates good vibrations.

In support of the above findings, another study by Sandstrom and Dunn (2013) revealed how being our usual, efficiency-driven selves while buying our daily cup of coffee is robbing us of an opportunity to be happier. While we routinely rush through the transaction without so much as a smile, the study found that people who smiled and engaged in a brief conversation with the barista experienced more positive feelings than those who stuck to the impersonal, efficient approach.

These studies have two main findings. First, we tend to *think* or *assume* we're better off keeping to ourselves than having short interactions with strangers. Second, we're wrong about the first point. The simple act of engaging people in short bursts has been shown to make us happier and more inclined to be social, and it will also help us mentally and psychologically warm up to be our best in conversations and small talk no matter the context.

There seems to be a question of inertia. As we go through our days, we're typically a little caught up in our own heads, or distracted with whatever we're doing. It's as though the default setting is to be turned "off" socially. What does this tell us? That if we want to become more sociable, master the art of conversation, make more friends, or simply be that person who can easily make people laugh and like them, then we need to find a way to move ourselves out of this antisocial mode. We need to become more comfortable and skilled at being "on" socially—a bit like a well-trained athlete might find it easier to start running than someone who hasn't run for years!

We need to engage in more short interactions—or what researcher Steven Handel calls "ten-second relationships"— with others, because they have the potential to boost our moods, change our perspectives, and warm us up socially. It's as though these interactions keep the social engagement engine running. If you're out of practice, small interactions like this might seem pointless or even aggravating, but remember, you might be completely biased and incorrect in this belief. Also remember that even if you crave "big talk" with people, you inevitably have to move through the smaller talk first.

Of course, though we may now recognize the benefits of short interactions, it's still understandable how the thought of striking up a conversation with a total stranger may be uninviting or even repulsive to those of us who aren't social butterflies. We feel ill-equipped to engage in fruitful social interactions, so we prefer the loneliness of keeping to ourselves.

But if this is your knee-jerk response to approaching people cold or striking up conversations with strangers, just remind yourself that you have a natural bias to assume that you prefer keeping to yourself. You can probably recall a situation where you were glad you reached out and engaged with someone, even if you were reluctant at first. A lot of people hate small talk simply because shifting gears into socializing mode can feel awkward or uncomfortable. But they forget that, once warmed up, the benefits far outweigh the initial costs. It's a bit like exercise in the morning. Sure, it takes your muscles time to warm up, but you soon start to enjoy yourself, and gain the benefits of physical activity.

How do we counter our natural tendency to avoid small interactions and warm ourselves up for routinely conversing with others? How do we get into the habit of being interested in people and build enough social confidence so we can turn that interest into meaningful interactions?

Well, that's part of the logic behind only trying for ten-second interactions. It's practice! And what you practice will become easier and more natural with time. Hey, you can make it one second (*Hello there!*) or five seconds (*Hi, how's your day going? Great to hear, bye!*) depending on your level of comfort. But keep the goal small and stay consistent.

Wondering where to find willing subjects for your small talk practice? Luckily, they're all around you. You constantly encounter multiple opportunities for warming up to interactions and building your social confidence. For instance, think of your typical day. On your way to work, how many people do you spend at least some time ignoring, whether those you pass by on the street, sit with on your commute, or stand beside in elevators? Greet at least one of those people with *"Good morning"* and offer either a compliment (*"Nice coat. The fabric looks cozy."*), an observation (*"The sky's cloudless today. Looks like the showers are letting up."*), or a question (*"I see you're reading John Grisham. Which of his novels is your favorite?"*).

For lunch, do you eat solo, hunched over your work desk? Try instead to spend your lunch hour someplace with shared seating, such as your office pantry or a nearby picnic area. Sit beside a colleague you always see in your building yet never got the chance to talk to, and get the conversation rolling by asking about recent company events (*"I heard your department is starting a new leg of research. How's it going?"*).

Finally, as you pick up groceries on your way home, chat with another shopper mulling over products in the same grocery aisle you're in (*"I saw this sauce in an online recipe. Have you tried cooking with it?"*). At the checkout counter, smile and greet the cashier (*"How's your shift going so far?"*). This segment of society is especially suited to help you practice and warm up—in fact, they don't really have much of a choice. Baristas. Cab drivers. Cashiers. The grocery bag boy. Waiters. Doormen. Valets. You get the picture!

Their job performance depends on their customer service skills, and if they want to keep their jobs, they have to be courteous to you. This alone should eliminate the fear you have of crashing and burning in any social interaction, because, well, it's their job to prevent that and probably laugh at your jokes. You'll see that crashing and burning is never really that bad, and people move on quickly—they'll probably forget the interaction within the next ten minutes.

There's also typically a captive audience behind the store counter or cash register. These employees are usually stuck being stationary in a position for long periods of time, and for those who have held the above jobs… you know that it's not the most thrilling life. Most of the time, they are bored out of their minds, so having someone engage them will be a positive experience for them. You will make their day pass faster and just give them something to do. You might be the only one to treat them with respect and show actual interest in them as a person, which would undoubtedly make you the highlight of their day. In other words, they'll be glad to talk to you.

With service people, you can test different stories, reactions, phrases, greetings, facial expressions, and so on. It's a low-risk way to test the waters. Unless you offend them in a deeply personal way, these people will still be courteous to you, but you can gauge how positive their reactions are to all of your tactics to know what works best. You can continuously improve and hone your skills. You can witness your progress with future interactions. As you see their reactions change, you can fine-tune what you're doing and keep stepping up your game.

Essentially, you're in a *safe environment to practice and polish your social skills* without fear of any judgment or consequences. More than that, you can learn to read people, process their signals, and calibrate your interactions to different types of people. This is a process that takes trial and error, but you can speed it up exponentially by engaging with the people you come across. Even if you do put your foot in it somehow, chances are the interaction is over quickly and the fallout minimal.

So, make it a goal to initiate and create a ten-second interaction with a stranger each day, and especially on the way to functions, events, and parties. This will warm you up for conversation and build the habit of being interested in people.

Reading Out Loud

Think of it this way: conversation is a bit like a race, and you have to warm up and prepare yourself accordingly (or pull the proverbial muscle and have to drop out . . .).

When we want our best race, whether athletic or academic, we always engage in some type of warm-up. It's almost common sense at this point that you need to prime your body and mind to the kind of performance that you want. Runners stretch, singers sing scales. What about people engaging in conversation? Well, you might be surprised by how much your speaking muscles need help and how much getting them in shape can make you instantly more charismatic. Recall back in grade school when you weren't paying attention, the teacher called on you, and you had to spend five seconds clearing your throat while still sounding meek and awkward because you weren't prepared. That's what we are seeking to eliminate, as well as imbue you with a sense of confidence.

To warm up your conversation skills, you just need to do something we've done almost every day in our lives: **read out loud**.

It sounds simple, but reading out loud this time will be different from any other time you've previously done it because now, you will have a purpose. I've provided an excerpt from the *Wizard of Oz*, which is in the public domain, for those copyright police out there. If this doesn't pique your interest, you can feel free to find your own excerpt. Just try to make sure there is a multitude of emotions included, preferably with dialogue from different characters. Here it is:

After climbing down from the china wall the travelers found themselves in a disagreeable country, full of bogs and marshes and covered with tall, rank grass. It was difficult to walk without falling into muddy holes, for the grass was so thick that it hid them from sight.

However, by carefully picking their way, they got safely along until they reached solid ground. But here the country seemed wilder than ever, and after a long and tiresome walk through the underbrush they entered another forest, where the trees were bigger and older than any they had ever seen.

"This forest is perfectly delightful," declared the Lion, looking around him with joy. "Never have I seen a more beautiful place."

"It seems gloomy," said the Scarecrow.

"Not a bit of it," answered the Lion. "I should like to live here all my life. See how soft the dried leaves are under your feet and how rich and green the moss is that clings to these old trees. Surely no wild beast could wish a pleasanter home."

"Perhaps there are wild beasts in the forest now," said Dorothy.

"I suppose there are," returned the Lion, "but I do not see any of them about."

They walked through the forest until it became too dark to go any farther. Dorothy and Toto and the Lion lay down to sleep, while the Woodman and the Scarecrow kept watch over them as usual.

Seems like an easy task, right? Go ahead and try to read the above excerpt out loud to yourself. Don't be shy. If you actually did it, you'll notice that you do literally feel warmed up and readier to keep speaking and conversing after just using your vocal cords for a bit. Vocal cords are, after all, muscles too. But that's just the beginning. Now comes the instruction.

Pretend like you are reading the excerpt out loud to a class of second graders. Read the excerpt like you're giving a performance in a contest, and the winner is judged on how emotional and ridiculous they can be! Pretend you're a voice actor for a movie trailer and you have only your voice to get a wide range of emotion across. Go over the top as much as possible—which, granted, won't be much at first.

Exaggerate every emotion you can find to the tenth degree. Scream parts of it loudly while whispering softly in other parts. Use different and zany voices for different characters. Here's your chance to try some accents out. Make any laughter maniacal, make any rage boiling, make any happiness manic—you get the idea. For that matter, what emotions are you picking up in the text? Even in such a short excerpt, there are emotional high and low points. Find them, or create them, and make them sound like climaxes to stretch your range of emotion.

Pay attention to your voice tonality. Are you accustomed to using a monotone? Would someone be able to tell what the character or narrator is thinking or trying to convey by listening to you? Use the excerpt to practice your range of vocal expressiveness—try to embody the term *emotional diversity*. Go ahead and try it for the second time with all this newfound instruction (preferably while alone unless you don't mind getting some serious side eye).

Did you hear a difference? Here is some additional instruction: pay attention to your diction and how you enunciate. Your tongue, too, is a muscle. In a sense, you are literally warming your tongue up so you don't stutter or stumble on your words when you talk to others. This is another reason to have an excerpt with dialogue—the more diversity of the text you are reading, the better warmed up you will be. If you have the habit of muttering like a curmudgeon, put a stop to it and make sure you are speaking and articulating your words as clear as a bell.

Pay attention to your breathing. Do you feel like you're running out of breath? It's because your diaphragm is weak and not used to projecting or sounding confident. That's the reason singers put their hands on their stomachs—it's to check that their diaphragms are engaged. Try it and make sure that your stomach is taut and tight. Sit up straight and open up your body. Picture the breath in your lungs feeding the words coming from your mouth and play around with how to control its release gradually.

The point here is to literally breathe life into the words that you are speaking. Those who speak without their diaphragm inevitably come off as quiet, meek, and mouse-like. Running out of air at the end of a sentence can signal anxiety—or make your listeners anxious on your behalf. But the better you can project your voice, the wider the emotional range you can create.

Another key element of how you say something is, of course, your pacing—the speed at which you talk. Your speaking speed can either be your friend or undermine what you're trying to say. Rate of speech can imply an emotion all by itself—for instance, when making a big point, you should slow down your pace to allow the impact to be felt. If you use the wrong speed or your pacing is off, a lot of what you have to say can easily be lost or confused and misinterpreted. Rushing can make you seem stressed or unconfident, speaking to slow will likely bore people. But just the right pauses here and there can add real depth and nuance to the way you're perceived.

Ready to read through the excerpt one more time? Try again, but this time, make sure you're utilizing everything you just read about breath, pace, and tone. Now compare your third version to the first version you did without any instruction. *That's* the difference between warming yourself up and not, and most likely. Importantly, the first version is how you're probably coming across the vast majority of the time. Potentially flat or weak. Hopefully, this exercise has illustrated to you just how much of a difference you can make with warming up alone.

The added bonus is that while you are feeling silly and over the top, you are actually stretching your limits in terms of emotional and vocal expressiveness. The simple act of getting out of your comfort zone, even in private, will stretch your boundaries and make you more expressive and confident sounding in general. All this from reading out loud? Yes, if done with purpose and deliberation!

Choose a Role Model

No matter how charismatic or charming you feel you are, you probably started with a role model in mind—even just a general picture of who you wanted to be. I make no secret of the fact that I treat Will Smith's character from *The Fresh Prince of Bel Air* as my role model. *The Fresh Prince of Bel Air* was a television show that ran from 1990-1996 and lives on through constant reruns.

Seeing that show and the main character was one of the first instances where I took notice of how someone interacted differently with people, and I wanted to create that feeling too.

So why the Fresh Prince?

To me, he is simply the epitome of a charismatic personality.

He says what he wants, is amazingly likeable, is comfortable being the center of attention, is confident to the point of being arrogant, can verbally spar with anyone, and is flat-out hilarious. Because of how much people like him and his presence, he gets away with far more than he should be able to, and can generally use charm to shape his life.

It was amazing. Of course, I knew it was a television show and people were scripted to react to him with positivity, but you can give the same script to one hundred people and ninety-nine of them won't come close to the delivery and presence Will Smith had. Again, I knew it was a television show, but it still felt realistic in how charisma like that would affect people in a positive manner.

When I was first starting to diligently figure out the kind of person I wanted to evolve into, the Fresh Prince was an important concept for me. Since he embodied many of the things I wanted, I was able to grow, albeit sometimes in a forced and artificial way, closer to my personal ideal simply by asking myself one question:

What would the Fresh Prince do?

The next technique we'll look at is how you can ask what your charismatic role model would do in any social situation. I know, it's a little cheesy. You might feel like you are doing a pale imitation at first, but soon you will find your true voice as a synthesis of your personality and what elements from your role model suit you—that's why this chapter is about finding *your* role model, and not just using mine.

Putting yourself in someone's shoes has a surprising number of benefits for growing your sense of charisma. It's a powerful question to ask yourself for a few reasons.

First, asking what your role model would do in that particular social situation diverts your attention from the situation at hand.

When we are too focused on a situation, it is too personal, or we are too invested, it suddenly becomes very difficult to make a decision because the stakes seem so high, and the consequences seem so large. For example, it's near impossible for us to abide by the amazing advice we dole out to our friends because we can't assess our own situations objectively. It's far easier to give advice, act, and even be charismatic when we are detached from the outcome and can think about it without fear or anxiety playing a part.

In other words, when you divert your attention from yourself and onto your role model, you remove a lot of the social pressure that keeps you from saying what you really want to, or acting in a way that you are scared to. Viewing social situations through an objective, relatively impersonal perspective by framing it through someone else will allow you to analyze the social situation you are in and calibrate your next move.

The more you ask yourself this question, the more habitual and second nature it will become, which is positive because you will essentially be able to condition yourself in the heat of the moment to act reflexively.

Second, having a charisma role model (or three) in mind allows you to understand how you actually want to be.

For instance, perhaps you want to develop more confidence and be more outspoken in social situations. In that case, you might ask yourself what someone like Robert Downey,

Jr. would do. For another trait you want to develop—for example, a razor-sharp sense of wit and humor—perhaps you could ask yourself what Conan O'Brien would do (again, these are just my examples, you might have completely different people in mind).

Everyone has different strengths and weaknesses, and has a different conception of how they want to be perceived. Not everyone fits the extrovert ideal of magnetic charisma, and that's perfectly fine. Not everyone wants to fit that ideal, either. So, who fits you best in terms of what you aspire to?

Men: Tyler Durden, Don Draper, Charles Xavier, Jack Donaghy, Ari Gold, John Wayne.

Women: Sheryl Sandberg, Jennifer Lawrence, Michelle Obama, Hilary Clinton, Sarah Silverman, Tina Fey.

The list could go on forever because we are not all looking for the same thing. You might even have a real-life friend or family member on that list that inspires you, or a blend of a few key personalities you've encountered throughout your life. But just the act of going through this exercise should inform you as to what you feel your weaknesses are, the ways you want to be perceived, and what you ultimately feel you are missing. Get the feeling and essence of the person and how they work on the inside, rather than imitating their exact behaviors.

I would encourage you to choose a handful of role models for charisma, and then list out three specific traits you like from each of them. For instance, Robert Downey Jr.: (1) witty, (2) irreverent, and (3) brutally confident. Most of our charismatic role models will have quite a lot in common with each other, and it will allow you to see the traits that you are really chasing.

This chapter is about choosing people that excel in areas that you currently do not, and embodying them to make their reactions your habits.

Third, getting into the habit of asking what your role model would do is like donning a mask or playing a role. If you've ever acted on stage, in front of a camera, or even dressed up for Halloween, you may have noticed how differently you feel. You're not quite yourself, and that is an extremely empowering feeling.

When you're not yourself and are immersed in a mask or role, you can say and think things that you wouldn't dare to otherwise. This happens because you are literally thinking through another perspective and becoming detached from yours, and also because you know in the back of your mind that you are safe from repercussions. There's a reason that Halloween is associated with pranks, riots, and crime — because people relish the fact that they are in different roles and can do things they've always wanted to without consequence.

You feel safe, you feel empowered, and you feel confident, because it's not necessarily *you* that you are channeling; it's your role model.

Now, you're probably wondering how this reconciles, again, with not being fake or trying too hard to be the cool guy. The secret is this: by incorporating your role model's characteristics, you actually end up portraying a totally unique blend of characteristics that is *one hundred percent you*. Remember, you identified your role model specifically because you admired and valued those traits—in other words, they are a part of you already, because you gravitated toward those traits and not others. As part of you (albeit a small, undeveloped part) wants to be like that, or sees something of yourself in that other person. If you use this technique successfully, what you ultimately do is use your role models as a kind of bootstrap to discover your *own* hidden traits.

Obviously, the end result is not that I closely resemble the Fresh Prince—in fact, nobody would guess that he was my inspiration. Rather, by using his persona as a step on the ladder, I make it a little easier to be more like myself.

Pick a few difficult or confusing situations you may have stuck in your head from the past few weeks. What did you do? Now, how would your role model have responded, instead? Document these, rehearse them mentally, and run through them periodically so you are able to start *thinking* like your role model instead of just emulating them. There's a big difference, isn't there? Logically, after the fact, you are able to come up with these differences, but again, it's difficult to fight against your emotions and fears in the heat of the moment.

In a sense, asking, "What would they do?" becomes a safe place for you to retreat you when you are in an unfamiliar social situation. In time, you stop having to ask yourself this deliberately because you end up doing it automatically. You are no longer pretending to be someone with confidence—you really do have confidence.

The notion of choosing a role model is not only socially proven, but also has roots in the psychology of learning.

It's known as *modeling*, and it is a method where people learn by observation and subsequent imitation alone, without instruction or explicit guidance. Patients and clients have been taught skills, behaviors, and habits just through modeling for decades—which means that finding your role model is more powerful than you probably imagined.

Modeling accounts for how we learned social cues, social norms, and even how to act at the dinner table. The landmark study on modeling and social learning was known as the Bobo Doll Experiment, conducted by Albert Bandura in 1961. In the experiment, children observed adults acting aggressively toward a Bobo doll—a doll which springs back upright after it is knocked down. One group of children observed the adults being rewarded after knocking the Bobo doll down, and subsequently began to model and imitate their aggressive behavior.

Granted, the Bobo doll experiment didn't have very flattering conclusions because of the behavior modeled, but it does suggest that if we choose positive role models, we can and will begin to adopt that behavior as our own, with time.

Life is a Series of Stories

No, seriously. We don't think of our lives as being very interesting on a day-to-day basis, but we do quite a bit more than we realize. Do you think that you're a boring person? Do you sometimes freeze when a stranger asks you something about yourself, suddenly going blank at the prospect of having to say something interesting? It's probably because you have the small, day-to-day view of yourself, rather than the expanded narrative—the more interesting big picture.

Imagine the most interesting person you know. They might seem like fascinating people, but if you picked any random Tuesday morning to drop in on their lives, it probably wouldn't be all that exciting. It's only when you zoom out a little that the full narrative of their life looks more coherent, more engrossing. Have you ever noticed that an event seems to get bigger, funnier or more interesting only afterwards, when you tell it? The interest is in the *telling*. It's all in how the story is told.

This fact, combined with the fact that nothing stops a conversation cold quite like a one-word answer, means that you should strive to present your life as a series of mini stories. Keep in mind that we're not talking about becoming good at stand up or fashioning a massive epic sage for yourself, quite the contrary. It's more about connecting with others by using mini stories about the small details in every day of your life.

What is the definition of a mini story in this context?

"So what do you do?"
"I'm a marketing executive."
"Oh, cool. Well, I'm going to find the bathroom now."

Let's try again.

"So what do you do?"
"I'm a marketing executive. I deal mostly with clients. Just last week we had a crazy client that threatened to send his bodyguards to our office! I definitely wish I dealt more with the creative side."
"Oh my God! Did he actually send them?"

That's a mini story. It's answering questions briefly using the elements of a story—an action that occurs to a subject with some sort of conclusion. As you can see above, a brief mini story will create exponentially more conversation and interest than any answer to the question "What do you do?" All you needed was three sentences. And this is all you need to make yourself an exponentially more captivating conversationalist.

Yes, the technically correct answer is in the first exchange, and you probably have it stored away in your mind that your occupation is, in fact, a marketing executive. But good conversationalists learn the knack of presenting even boring information as an engrossing story. When people make small talk with you and ask you small talk questions, they probably aren't interested in your one-word answers or boring recaps of boring weekends. They *want* to hear something interesting, so give it to them.

Not only that, stories are an inside view to the way you think and feel. They're a foot in the door. Learning those about you is the first step in allowing anyone to relate and feel connected to you, so it's imperative that you learn how to take a closed-ended question and expand it to your advantage. The great thing is it gives you an opportunity to run with the story in any direction you like. You can play up any aspect of the story, divert away from one aspect, or introduce a completely new theme. It's up to you. Using a mini story will also encourage them to reciprocate, and suddenly trading war stories from college parties is on the table.

It doesn't have to be complicated. When you break down what a mini story actually needs to be compelling, they become much simpler to make on the spur of the moment. What's great about mini stories is you can also create these *before* a conversation so you can have compelling anecdotes at hand in response to very common and widespread questions. The main benefit to creating mini stories ahead of time is to be able to avoid one-word answers that you may be accustomed to using.

I would implore you to cue up similar mini stories of roughly three sentences in length for some of the most common conversation topics that will arise, such as:

1. Your occupation (If you have a job that is unusual or nebulous, make sure that you have a layman's description of your job that people can relate to.)
2. Your week
3. Your upcoming weekend
4. Your hometown
5. Your hobbies and so on

When you are using a mini story to answer a question, make sure to first acknowledge the question that was asked. Remember, you don't want anything to appear rehearsed or fake. But then, realizing that you have something far more interesting to say, you can jump into the mini story, which should be able to stand by itself.

"How was your weekend?"
"It was fine. I watched four Star Wars movies."
"Okay, I'm going to go talk to someone else now."

Let's try again.

"How was your weekend?"
"It was fine, but did I tell you about what happened last weekend? A dog wearing a tuxedo walked into my office."

"Wait. Tell me more."

Using mini stories allows you to avoid the tired back of forth of "Good, how about you" you'll find in everyday small talk. That's the first step to being captivating.
Mini stories also underscore the importance of providing more details, as mentioned in an earlier chapter, and avoiding one-word answers.

Details provide a three-dimensional description of you and your life. That automatically makes people more interested and invested because they are already painting a mental picture in their minds and visualizing everything.

Details also give people more to connect to, think about, and attach themselves to. With more details, there is a substantially higher likelihood that people will find something funny, interesting, in common, poignant, curious, and worthy of comment. You'll seem more human, and it will be easier for people to identify with and empathize with you.

Detail and specificity put people into a specific place and time. It allows them to imagine exactly what's happening and start caring about it. Think about why it's so easy to get sucked into a movie. We experience enormous sensory stimulation and almost can't escape all of the visual and auditory detail, which is designed to get us invested in the outcome. Detailed stories and conversations are inviting others to share a mental movie with you—and the invitation itself can be a subtle signal that you'd like to introduce just that tiny bit extra closeness into the conversation.

Beyond giving flavor to your conversation and storytelling, and giving the other person something to ask about, details are important because they are what make people emotionally engaged. Details remind people of their own lives and memories and make them feel more drawn to whatever is presenting them. People love to hear themselves reflected in others' stories. Details can compel others to laugh, feel mad, feel sad, or feel surprise. It sounds grandiose, but stories really can control moods and emotions.

For example, if you include details about specific songs that played during your high school dances, it's likely that someone will have memories attached to those songs and become more emotionally interested in your story. There is no such thing as TMI—too much information. Share details about all the figurative nooks and crannies, because that's what makes you interesting on an emotional level.

Plumping up Your Conversation Resume

Previous points in this chapter about pre-conversation have centered around your psychology and your physiology. In other words, to hit the ground running and have great conversations, you've got to find ways to put yourself in the mood for them. This means warming and loosening up your vocal cords, as well as getting gout of your rut and allowing yourself to connect to others genuinely, for example with mini stories. However, we haven't covered what to actually say yet, have we? This is when we rectify that.

As mentioned before, conversation isn't always about thinking quickly on your feet in the heat of the moment. That's an entirely different skill that can be trained, but what's easier and more useful on a daily basis is to create for yourself a *conversation résumé,* which you can draw from in nearly every conversation.

What the heck does this mean? It means that when you're in the heat of a conversation, and an awkward silence is looming, sometimes we stress and our minds blank completely. We try to think on our feet, but our feet are frozen to the floor. A conversation résumé comes to the rescue because it is basically an annotated overview of who you are. It's a brief list of your best and funniest stories, your notable accomplishments, your unique experiences, and viewpoints on salient and topical issues. It allows you to keep your best bits ready for usage.

It's no different from a résumé you would use for a job interview—but with a very different purpose in mind here. Know your personal talking points, rehearse them, and be ready to unleash them whenever necessary, with ease. However, just like in a job interview, having this résumé allows you to present the version of yourself that you most want. You might need to adapt it slightly depending on the situation, but it's a conversational tool kit that you can always rely on.

It may seem inconsequential to have such thoughts prepared, but imagine how excruciating the silence is in a job interview when you have to scramble, think of an answer on the fly, and say it while knowing it's generic or useless. It's simply the difference between having a good answer or story when someone asks, "What did you do last weekend?" versus simply saying, "Oh, not too much. Some TV. What about you?" How about how few of us can answer the following without stuttering and stalling: "So what's your story?" The conversation résumé allows you to remind yourself that you're not such a boring person after all and that people should have reason to be interested in you.

As we mentioned earlier, we're not naturally in this state of mind. We generally don't think of ourselves in terms of sound bites but just expect that in the moment, we'll think of something. But developing and constantly updating your conversation résumé can save you from awkward silences and make it supremely easy to connect with others. It's like a way to quickly move through those beginning phases of small talk, putting you and the other person more quickly at ease.

It may feel difficult to come up with right now, but imagine how much easier it is without the stress of someone staring at you, waiting for your reply. It's this process of mental preparation that will translate to real conversational success. What you come up with on your résumé won't always make it into everyday conversation, but the more you have it on your brain, the more it will, and the more captivating you will appear become. Have you ever been told by good friends that they had no idea how awesome you were until they got to know you a bit better? That's a sure-fire clue that you could benefit from have a solid conversation résumé.

There are four sections to your conversation résumé, and it's not a bad idea to update them every couple of weeks. Admittedly, you may never have thought to answer any of these questions before, which means they definitely aren't coming through in conversation. Don't sell yourself short!

Daily life:

- What did you do over the weekend? Anything notable?
- How is your week/day going? Anything notable?
- How is your family/significant other? Anything notable?
- How is work going? Anything notable?

Personal:

- What are your hobbies? Anything notable?
- What's your biggest passion or interest outside of work? Anything notable?
- Where are you from? Anything notable?
- How long have you lived at your current location and worked at your current job? Anything notable?
- Where did you go to school and what were you involved in? Anything notable?
- What do you do for work? Anything notable?

Notable:

- What are your five most unique experiences?
- What are your five most personally significant accomplishments?

- What are ten strengths—things you are above average at, no matter how big or small?
- Name ten places you have traveled in the past five years.
- Name the past five times you have gone out to a social event.
- Name ten things you cannot live without—don't take this question too literally. It is asking about your interests.

Staying Current:

- What are the top five current events of the week *and* month? Learn the basics and develop an opinion and stance on them.
- What are four funny personal situations from the past week? Be able to summarize them as a brief story.
- What are the four most interesting things you've read or heard about in the past week? Be able to summarize them as a brief story.

If you've ever felt like your mind was going blank, this is the cure. There are so many pieces of information that you've just dug out of yourself that it should be nearly impossible to run out of things to say. Occasionally update your anecdotes, and tweak those that don't get good feedback— you don't want to end up saying the same stories over and over!

Why not do a quick run through as well as a vocal warm up exercise so you feel relaxed, confident, and prepared? Remember to review this before you head into socially intense situations, and you will be able to keep up with just about anyone. You just may realize that while some people appear to be quicker than lightning, they may simply remember more about themselves at that moment.

Takeaways

- To be a better conversationalist and a small talk natural, it makes sense to prepare. Before you even have a conversation, make sure that you're in the right mindset. This may take practice.
- Use "barista practice" to help you get warmed up and into the socializing

mindset. We naturally assume we will dislike connecting with others, when research shows the opposite. But we can get rusty! Barista practice is finding ways to have one- to ten-second-long mini-interactions with waiters, cashiers and service staff to get yourself in the small talk habit.

- Reading out loud is an exercise that can help you physically warm your vocal cords and get you feeling comfortable in your own voice. Read a chosen passage out loud with as much variability in emotion, tone, pitch, accent, pace, and volume to stretch your expressive powers and get you feeling confident and warmed up.

- Another way to boost confidence as you're learning to improve small talk skills is to fashion a role model that you then emulate. Ask what they would do in any socially tense situation, and what exact traits they have that you admire. The psychological distance and sense of safety can be just what you need to bootstrap those traits in yourself.

- Many of us feel like we are boring and don't have anything interesting to say, or we freeze when asked questions. A great approach is to think in terms of telling mini stories to engage interest and capture the emotional investment of your audience.

- Prepare beforehand by thinking of a few potential mini stories to share when prompted with questions—a few sentences are enough. This can be thought of as a conversational résumé and will help you avoid awkward silences or freezing and not knowing what to say.

Chapter 3. Set the Mood

Divulging

Remember the boring and annoying know-it-all? The "technically correct" person who brags or shows off? Good conversational chemistry is not made from fascinating facts or impressive feats. It's an *emotional* experience—people bond over how they feel in one another's company, and not strictly on the content they exchange.

Sharing more about yourself can make others like you more. The principle of self-disclosure involves disclosing information about yourself to make people more interested and emotionally invested in you. It can also make people feel closer to you and more open to sharing things about themselves in exchange. Sharing things about yourself works because it makes you become a real three-dimensional human they can relate to and feel familiar with. When you self-disclose, others will, too, and that's where you really start to break through barriers.

You've probably experienced this already. You might have been on casual acquaintance terms with someone, but one day, you feel the relationship takes a step forward somehow. Why? It's usually because one or both of you has taken a step to reveal themselves emotionally, and to open up. The problem is, most people don't do this off the bat. Like in the first principle, you must make the first move and start disclosing things about yourself to encourage the other person to do so. Sadly, the responsibility to initiate likability again falls on you.

Sharing More

Now you may wonder just what to share. What kind of information should you impart? What information is TMI (too much information) and hence will make people not like you? What information is beneficial to share with others and enhances your likability? What should you keep private? People err on the side of appearing mysterious, in control, and invulnerable. (Remember the cool guy? This is him again.)

I'm going to tell you something that may rankle your inner Cool Guy: Generally, the more you disclose, the better. TMI is actually beneficial for your likability because, again, this is how friends relate. Friends are notorious for oversharing without shame or inhibition. They may laugh, gag, or declare, "I didn't need to know that!" But they still share everything. The sharing, in fact, is a sign of closeness, trust, and familiarity. There's an old piece of advice that says that if you want to befriend someone, start by acting as if they already *are* your friend. It works because we switch from being guarded and carefully measured, and instead relax and reveal our true, lovably imperfect selves.

So even if you feel that you are entering TMI territory, that is still better than not disclosing anything because you are still treating others like your friends. And you still stand out in people's memories as someone genuine, unusual, and noteworthy—in other words, human is better than perfect!

Socializing can be scary. It's not easy to share yourself with others because there is always the threat, real or perceived, that you will be judged or disliked. We may not even realize that to counter this anxiety, we put a subtle wall around ourselves, being careful never to appear too emotional or even weak. But this is actually the opposite of how it is. By *under* sharing, you present a version of yourself who is afraid to make any waves . . . and is ultimately very forgettable. In fact, many people find themselves not really liking those people are agreeable and generic and bland. Perhaps they can sense that the whole personality is not fully present?

Share what is on your mind. TMI might include details of your sex life or your controversial opinions that will offend or alienate people. In polite conversation with strangers, these details are not appropriate. But friends love to cross polite boundaries, so to put both this principle and the first one into play, overshare on things you normally would not share with strangers to gain more leverage and likability with others. Share slowly at first to gauge people's responses, but once you get the sense that someone is on the same page and willing to befriend you as well, you can open the floodgates, so to speak.

The more you reveal about yourself, the more connection points you generate with the other person. You reveal things you like or dislike, which the other person may be able to relate to and disagree or agree with. You can find more things in common as you reveal your preferences, opinions, loves, hates, likes, dislikes, sensitivities, memories, emotions, thoughts, and anecdotes. If you are unsure of whether a particular anecdote is genuinely too much, err on the side of making fun of yourself, revealing an unflattering secret or stating an outrageous but generally harmless opinion or memory. In other words, if you target somehow, it's best to target *yourself*.

For example, say you are at a party and meeting with people you have never seen before. Usually this situation is daunting and you feel awkward and clam up with a drink in your hand to protect your fragile ego from rejection by these new people. But using the tips in this book, you disclose a lot about yourself and you talk about how much you like fishing, anime, and knitting, all three of your seemingly unrelated hobbies. You have stories about each of these that you can launch into from normal small talk questions. They speak to your interests, how you react to situations, and your personality in general.

Everyone in the room who loves one of those three things (or can simply relate to how you might react to a situation) can now connect with you, and a conversation is born based on the topic you two share. All you needed to do was answer questions with a series of details about yourself or tell a story about yourself. In this case, you don't even have to take any risks by revealing something personal; you simply have to volunteer more information than is strictly required.

Think about it this way: provide three details where you would have replied with a one-word answer, or provide three sentences where you would have replied with one sentence. That's the basic type of step that is needed for self-disclosure to work its wonders. If you had a boring weekend, still name three details so people aren't left with nothing to work with. It might feel extraneous at first, but it might also let you realize how little you disclose about yourself to others.

Share your emotions. The reason emotions are so powerful is because they are universal. Everyone in the world, from Americans to Aboriginals to African bush people, share similar emotions, emotional responses, and even facial expressions. Scientific studies have shown that people from different cultures can recognize what smiles and frowns mean, which indicates that all people feel and express emotions in similar ways.

So, expressing your emotions and making them known to others is a foolproof method to get others to feel close to you. You access more primal, universal and nonverbal ways to communicate. You become more human and relatable when you express your emotions. And others feel more comfortable expressing their own emotions and agreeing or disagreeing with how you feel once you dare to be open about your emotions. It's as though, in sharing your own self freely and confidently, you communicate to others that you will receive them in the same way, and that it's safe to be genuine with you in return. Again, this starts with talking about how happy or sad something makes you—that's all it takes to open a deeper dialogue.

It can be particularly effective to lean into the kinds of emotions that other people feel less inclined to share. For example, somebody sharing how happy they are about being newly wed to their dream partner will get good reactions from people, but perhaps they may respond more readily when you share an amusing but embarrassing story of something unusual that happened to you. We are all, to some extent, wearing social masks—if you can reveal emotions that temporarily give people a glimpse of the real, imperfect human underneath the mask, you will connect with people on a much more powerful level.

Share stories from your own life. Again, this makes you seem more real and three-dimensional. Even though it doesn't feel like it, we all go through similar circumstances and struggles every day. We all brush our teeth, hate waking up, and do some kind of work. You almost certainly have some part of your life story that others can relate to. This makes people feel closer to you and lets them laugh and talk about how they went through the same thing. Often, they will start to tell their stories based on yours.

We all have common experiences. We all remember when we learned to ride a bike, embarrassing moments in high school, or disasters in dating. Share your story with gusto to make it seem more engaging and entertaining. Finally, give people room to interject with their own stories so that they can feel as if they are participating and relating to you. You won't be as likable if you hog the spotlight and never let others talk. The purpose of sharing is to encourage mutual sharing, so don't keep things focused on you.

Ultimately, you want to just get into the habit of talking about yourself more and sharing things you wouldn't necessarily think about sharing right now. You can work on even just thinking out loud more. You seem more real and spontaneous to others and you ensure that others can relate to you. You create more conversations out of thin air.

It can be intimidating. You have been taught your whole life to be modest and even private. Now you are going against years of teachings. You may worry that you are bothering others or overstepping boundaries. You may wonder if anyone cares about your weird story or wants to know your opinion. But the thing is, you will find that people actually love it when you talk about yourself more and become more open—it's an invitation for *them* to be more genuine and relaxed. You will have an easier time capturing others' attention, forming bonds, and even having fun with others just because you talk about yourself more.

Be warned, though, that this isn't permission to focus on yourself to the detriment of the conversational flow. The obvious rules still apply: listen to others, ask questions, and share the floor rather than taking the opportunity to give a speech. The only time where sharing more is a bad move is if you dominate the conversation to do so—for example interrupting someone else's story so you can interject your own!

No Judging

If you are still on the fence about opening up about yourself, here are some scientific studies that support the value of doing so in social situations.

A 1989 study by Hilton and Fein set out to determine the cause of people's judgments, assumptions, and stereotyping. What made the brain immediately assign traits and a veritable backstory to some people versus others? Why were some people so quick to jump to conclusions?

It was found that the less information people had about a certain subject or person, the more they began to fill in the gaps with information that was stereotypical of a general representation. If I described someone who belonged to a country club, drove an expensive car, played tennis, and liked lacrosse, there's a very specific image you might conjure up. It's almost like other people become like Rorschach blots onto which we project our own biases and assumptions—the more vague the picture, the more room for our own personal interpretation to come into things.

To prevent stereotyping and being instantly judged, Hilton and Fein found that simply providing details about the subject completely unrelated to the stereotype in mind diluted the stereotype and made people more likely to trust and like others. The more detail about the person, the better, even if it was completely random. This worked to turn people from members of a homogenous group into unique individuals. When we have limited information, we assume a person is just the same as the most stereotypical representation that has those traits.

When we have more information about someone in any regard, we realize we can't define them by those one or two traits, and we cease stereotyping and judging. You can make people like you more, stereotype you less, and emotionally invest in you more by providing seemingly useless and nonsensical details about your life. Recall the example of the person who liked anime, knitting and fishing. If they were in the company of people that had unflattering assumptions about anime fans, the detail about fishing and knitting may go a long way to cancelling those out—they might realize, "oh, this is not a stereotype, this is a complex, even contradictory person!"

People like to make fun of TMI as a kind of social faux pas, but the reality is that TMI can ultimately make you more likable. Think about it, who do you like and trust more—the composed, high achieving, perfectly in control person who is nevertheless a little cool emotionally, or the person who is okay with their flaws, confident enough to share their opinions, and happy to reach out to you on an emotional level? Of course, preferably you share positive or at least neutral information about yourself.

You become less of a threat and more of a known quantity. People become less suspicious of you and are more willing to give you the benefit of the doubt. In other words, you start to seem like a friend! By sharing seemingly trivial information about yourself, you allow people to feel like they know you, and they stop making assumptions.

And again, it doesn't even matter if the details are relevant to your identity, career, nonthreatening nature, or life. You can share your preference of glasses brand, your favorite color, and perhaps where you went to school. The more information about you that is out there, the less readily people can judge and stereotype you, simply because you won't fit those stereotypes and assumptions anymore.

For example, what if we learned that the person who plays tennis and belongs to a country club was poor growing up and went to college on a tennis scholarship? Also, they drive a twenty-year-old car and prefer to eat burritos. Does that change your view of them? We certainly wouldn't stereotype and make more assumptions about them like we previously did. In fact, the additional information we've learned blows the doors off any category we could put them into. And in a sense, that's the goal: to make it impossible for us to fit into any broad category or generalization. People are only judging you based on what they *aren't* seeing of you.

With more information, people suddenly become three-dimensional and not the static character biographies we see in movies. They are suddenly part of a story, which is also compelling. We are humanized, and we eventually realize that all humans are complex amalgamations. We were never going to fit into a stereotype or box. In reality, you really haven't done anything profound. You haven't even given any information that's important or useful.

Oversharing to maximize likability works to get people to feel that they know different sides of you. An easy way to share more details is to get into the habit of offering unsolicited information. For instance, if someone asks about your weekend, don't resort to answering, "Good, how about yours?" A guideline I like to use is to give three of four distinct details when answering easy questions—in this way, you will get into the habit of giving people more information, which will make conversation flow better anyway. Here's an example of zero sharing, little information, and a high likelihood of judgment and stereotyping.

Where are you from?

Oklahoma. You?

If you don't know anything about a person besides the fact they are from Oklahoma, where does your mind automatically go? It goes to whatever your stereotypes about Oklahoma are. You don't know if this person was born there, raised there, or only lived there for a couple of years. You don't know what they feel about Oklahoma. You don't have the context to make a good judgment about them, and yet you do anyway. So, this one trait defines them in your mind.

Now, here's an example of why giving unsolicited information can be helpful.

Where are you from?

Oklahoma, but I was born in New York. My parents were originally from France and I grew up visiting France very frequently. Also, I have eight dogs.

Now attempt to put *this* person into a box. It's the same person as before, but it's nearly impossible because there is so much information about them that you simply have to take them as they are. By knowing more about them, they have become more humanized and interesting. You may even find yourself wanting to know more about them. Like, why on earth *eight* dogs?

The added benefit to sharing unsolicited information and more in general is you make it extremely easy for others to connect with you. When you spout off details about your life, it's easy for them to find common ground and know you as a person. If you divulge personal information or intimate details of your life, you'll also be appearing to take the first steps to building trust and showing vulnerability to others. The more that's out there, the more there is for people to hook on to and relate to.

In 1997, Arthur Aron found that sharing did more than simply make you less susceptible to judgment from others. It creates emotional closeness and investment. In fact, the more intimate and *invasive* the information, the better.

He split participants into two groups. One group questioned each other on thirty-six very specific and intimate questions, including personal vulnerabilities and insecurities. Sample questions were "What is your most terrible memory?" and "What is your most treasured memory?" It's impossible to not get personal when faced with these questions. The other group was tasked to ask each other only shallow small talk questions about their everyday lives.

It's not something people are comfortable doing, but the participants followed directions. We feel like we're offending people or showing too much of ourselves, which is frightening. But the participants who were tasked with asking each other sensitive and sometimes prying personal questions developed greater levels of trust, rapport, and mutual comfort with one another. They felt emotional closeness, even though they didn't know each other before the study. Here are some examples of the questions used:

1. Do you want to be famous? For what?

This tells you what a person really values or imagines themselves to be skilled at. This can reveal someone's deepest desires and fantasies.

2. If you were able to live up to ninety and save either the mind or body of a thirty-year-old, which thing would you want to save?

You learn whether someone values the physical or mental more. You also learn if someone is honest or not.

3. If you could change anything about how you were raised, what would you change?

Here you gain deep insight into someone's past and history. You learn about his or her regrets and if his or her childhood was happy. You may learn some deeply personal secrets about someone.

4. If you could wake up tomorrow with any one quality, what would that quality be?

This question enables you to learn what someone wants to be and what he or she values in a person. The person you are asking this question of will always answer with the quality that matters most to him or her—or perhaps the one thing they feel they lack.

5. Is there something that you have wanted to do for a long time? Why haven't you done it yet?

People all have dreams. They also have regrets. Asking someone this lets you uncover what he or she dreams of or what he or she regrets not doing. It also makes him or her like you more because you are essentially goading this person to live his or her dream before it's too late.

The other group, however, didn't develop this level of trust, confidence, and intimacy. They essentially remained at their initial level of emotional closeness. Aron proved that when *you* share information, the *receiving parties* will like you more and feel closer to you and reciprocate. In a way, effective small talk is anything but small—it represents quite a big leap we take in broaching the distance between being strangers and being close friends.

Finally, according to a study by Theodore Newcomb, people tend to like those who are similar to them. The *similarity-attraction effect* is where people are drawn to like people. Newcomb measured his subjects' views on things like sex and politics and then sorted them into a house to live together. The subjects who shared the same viewpoints were usually friendlier by the end of the study than those with dissimilar viewpoints.

To compound the results of Newcomb's study, another study conducted by researchers at the University of Virginia and Washington University in St. Louis found that Air Force recruits tended to get along better with those who shared their negative personality traits rather than their positive ones. Now, you don't necessarily have to agree. But here's the thing. You can only discover possible similarities when you self-disclose. So by sharing more about yourself, you can find things in common that make others like you more.

Even if you *don't* ultimately find anything in common, you will still be appreciated by others as frank, forthright and confident. You know all those characters and celebrities that people "love to hate"? The fact is that a genuine person is simply more likeable and appealing—even if you don't agree with them!

Self-Entertaining and Amusement

We'll move on now to something that we've already hinted at somewhat in the previous section. By sharing more and not being judgmental, we come across to others as confident in ourselves. We communicate the message, "Here I am, being myself. I am not concerned with how that looks to others, I'm just being who I am." It's an attitude that is intensely appealing because it is calm and reassured in itself. This isn't a person who is desperate for approval, or working hard to force the interaction one way or another. Rather, it's a person who is doing something that everyone wants to be a part of: having fun.

Self-amusement is what it sounds like— amusing yourself. Having a good time. Pursuing what is interesting and amusing to you, and chatting about things simply because you find them interesting. It's a subtle but definite difference between focusing on entertaining others, and focusing more on making yourself happy. Couples counsellors often suggest that people observe their partners doing something they're passionate about that doesn't involve them. Something about seeing someone happy, confident, and engrossed in life is attractive to us—we are drawn to them and want to be a part of their enjoyment.

Picture an informal social occasion, for example a group of friends meeting up or people out on the town having a good time. Now picture someone who finds the whole prospect anxiety inducing, and is really petrified of talking to strangers or people they don't know well. They do their best to dress up nice, they give themselves a pep talk before leaving home, and in the moment they do their very best to come across as charming, telling jokes, and talking loudly.

They're trying hard. Perhaps a little *too* hard. You can't put your finger on it, but you sense the person is not at all confident, no matter how much they seem to be forcing themselves to be otherwise. Everything about them feels a little manufactured and insincere. You get the feeling that all this socializing business is actually quite hard work for them. And this is turn leaves a bad taste—why are they trying so hard? Isn't everyone supposed to be having a good time?

It's obvious: you can't force yourself to be relaxed. You can't plan to be spontaneous. You can't pretend to be authentic. All of these are not just uncomfortable for other people, they're logically impossible. People sense the tension in you, the effort, and respond to *that*.

Picture someone else at the same social gathering. They just seem to be in the zone. They're vibing off other people, there's a good flow and lots of laughs, and everyone seems to be riffing off one another, spurring one another on and, well, enjoying themselves. There's a kind of magic happening. The difference? Nobody is *trying* to do anything. They're just doing it. In the moment, as they are. In a way, it's the difference between work and play. The difference between spontaneously jamming in the kitchen when you hear your favorite song, and performing a professionally choreographed piece you've practiced for months.

To be playful and loose in this way takes a mindset shift. We are all like this as children, but we can lose touch with this spirit as we grow older and learn the boring rules of how to engage with and appeal to others. But, what happens when you think of conversations not as stressful interviews, but as games? What happens when you treat others not as potential threats or people to impress, but as co-creators of a totally exciting new adventure?

The idea with self-amusement or self-entertainment is not to put your head in the clouds and selfishly pursue your own whims, but to allow connections to develop from a place of curiosity, fun and creativity—which you can start by indulging in all by yourself. Keep things light in tone and flowing. You are not seeking attention or being a loudmouth, you are simply being loose and allowing the conversation to flow where it goes, without being too attached to any outcome.

Unlike what we've discussed so far, this is more of a mindset than a technique—in fact, it's an *anti*-technique, since it's all about forgetting the rules and following what is interesting, pleasurable or compelling, rather than following a trusted formula.

Again, we see the power of genuineness, of the confidence to be vulnerable, and of remembering that engaging with others is supposed to feel good. So, how can you use this principle in your own social life to be better at small talk?

Be playfully curious. Don't do things because you should, do them because you genuinely want to see what happens if you do. A conversation has infinite possibilities, and can unfold in any direction—play around and see what happens when you do this, or do that. Be like a scientist—notice what's happening and ask questions about it. Experiment—say something and see how it lands. For fun, throw a wild card in there just to see how it plays out. By keeping things open-ended, you keep the conversation fresh and alive (not to mention you have fun).

Don't second-guess yourself. If you're constantly self-conscious about what you're saying, you're unable to respond authentically and spontaneously. Avoid self-censoring—within reason, say what you feel (here's the TMI again). It's not that you throw all social convention and etiquette out the window, just that you relax and be natural, even taking a risk now and then. Express yourself—what is needed in a conversation is *you*, as you genuinely are, not a script or performance.

Be a little assertive. You need to be polite and accommodating, yes. But don't make the mistake of assuming you have to be a pushover to win friends. Speak up, and don't be afraid to go against the grain. Take your time when you talk, share your honest opinions, and don't feel you have to go along with conversations or activities you don't enjoy. State your business with the confidence of someone who knows that difference isn't a threat—in fact, it can be a source of interest and value. This is the key to making the switch from performing to some kind of ideal of what you think you *should* be, and simply prioritizing the pleasure of being how you actually *are*. Big difference.

Be brave. Overthinking and overanalyzing kills that childlike spirit of curiosity and play. While you're busy turning over this or that in your head, the moment passes you by. Instead, throw the caution to the wind sometimes and just go with it. Trist the flow of the conversation and your ability to move with it. At first, you may feel like you're being a bit reckless, but again, reframe this as excitement and adventure—you don't know how things will pan out, and *that's a good thing*!

Forget about the rules. So many conversations are bad because, when you really think about it, they're not conversations at all. They're simply people parroting the same old tired script they always, while their true opinions and personalities are hidden somewhere else. Rules can make things feel stale and inauthentic. Instead, stop worrying about what you can and cannot say, and try to really be in the moment, on your feet. Think of it as conversational Zen: just be alive to the possibilities of each moment without clinging to the old habits, tropes and stereotypes we all fall back on. The good conversationalist is not some smooth talker who has mastered all the right tricks—he's more like the guy who knows he's best when unencumbered by tricks in the first place, and doesn't need them anyway.

Overall, it's a question of attitude. Yes, you're reading a book about small talk "rules" right now, but try not to forget that people are fascinating, and that engaging with them in conversation is fun—a lot of fun! The people we talk to are whole universes in themselves, with entirely different perspectives, experiences, and things to teach us. What could be more exciting than stepping into that world with them, if only for just a minute?

Takeaways

- Connection with others is a wonderful thing, but how do we set the mood? We need to create the conditions to make good conversational chemistry flow. One big way is to divulge information about ourselves voluntarily, to get the conversation moving along.
- Oversharing may seem like something to avoid, but there is plenty of research to suggest that honestly opening up to others actually makes them like and trust us more. You'll distinguish yourself from the automatic stereotypes by giving specific details about yourself, and make your life seem more interesting and compelling.
  - We can divulge both by revealing additional information or by confessing to how we feel, sharing a story or revealing something

unexpected about ourselves. People bond over emotional identification, so don't worry about appearing weak or vulnerable—divulging will actually encourage others to do the same and foster good rapport.

- When you're asked a question, try responding with three or four pieces of information. Try sharing mini stories about your experiences, your memories, your hopes and dreams.
- Oversharing is almost always a good idea, except if you are hogging the conversation to do it!
- Self-amusement and self-entertainment are not a technique but a mindset, and a shift from focusing on what you ought to do for others, onto your own experience in the conversation.
- We can develop this attitude in ourselves by staying curious and open-ended, thinking of conversations as play, refusing to self-censor or second guess ourselves, being a little more assertive and brave in our self-disclosure, and being genuine and

spontaneous rather than relying on old stuffy rules.

- With self-amusement, we come across as more relaxed, confident, and attractive to others. We are no longer desperately trying to win approval or attaching to any outcome, but experimenting to see what happens, and where the conversation goes. This flexible spirit is precisely what makes a conversation really "click."

Chapter 4. Interact and Participate Fully

Questions – An Underrated Superpower

The physicist and theorist Heisenberg famously said, "What we observe is not nature itself, but nature exposed to our method of questioning." In the realm of conversation, we can take this to mean that what we see when we engage with other people is not how they really are, but how they look in relation to how we talk to them, and the questions we pose. To put it bluntly, if you ask boring questions, you get boring answers. If you don't ask *any* questions— well, the person in front of you starts to look like nothing more than a blank.

With all this focus on our own mindset, our preparedness and our ability to set the mood, we can forget that we always have at hand a very effective technique for reaching others—just ask them! Questions initiate and move conversations along particular paths. They give you some control and direction, they help you show interest, and they help you genuinely connect to and understand the person in front of you. In fact, questions are so important that it's hard to imagine anyone getting far in conversations without them.

Here, we'll focus on the *emotional* rather than *informational* impact of questions. You are not asking someone something because you literally don't know the answer and want them to tell you. That's what Google is for. In that sense, the answer can be important, sure, but it's not all that's important Simply asking in the first place, and the way you ask, can also send a powerful message. This chapter is about participating fully in conversations, and the backbone of quality participation is to think like a scientist like Heisenberg, and *get curious*.

The first thing to understand: not all questions are created equally. We can group exchanges, and therefore questions, into three levels, according to their underlying purpose. The first is to exchange information (or learn), the second to exchange feelings and emotions (or get others to bond with and like us), and the third is to exchange values (ditto). It's worth knowing the difference, so you're clear on what kind of conversation you're having, and why. For example, the know-it-all from our first chapter makes a mistake in responding to other people's appeals for an exchange of emotion and feelings, by supplying factual information instead. This is the person who completely misses the point by focusing on the details and not shared emotional content.

The second thing to understand is that we need to master both the asking and the answering of questions, at the right level. Doing so makes us more likeable, more empathetic, and more successfully at connecting to others. Let's take a closer look at how to frame and interpret questions, to use them to their best advantage.

Just ask more. Chances are, you're simply not asking enough questions. Even emotionally intelligent people can fail to show enough curiosity for others. Maybe you're too busy thinking of yourself or stressed about the interaction (still egocentric!) or maybe you genuinely don't care enough to know the answer. Maybe you think questions make you look nosy or worse, unsure of yourself. But the opposite is true.

Harvard research by Alison Wood Brooks and colleagues showed that when people were instructed to ask more questions in a conversation, people rated them as more likable than those who asked fewer questions. Speed daters were also found to agree more readily to a second date if their first date was filled with plenty of questions.

Don't be worried about coming off badly; the truth is that questions unlock the next level of human connection, and may even be more powerful in situations where questions are *not* expected, such as job interviews. They show that you're paying attention, that you care, that you're engaging in the situation proactively, that you have your own values and expectations, that you appreciate the opinion of the other person (otherwise, you wouldn't be asking for it) and that you have been listening. Not bad for a single line!

The Socratic Method

The kind of questions and the way they're delivered matters, of course. And, unfortunately, it's not just up to you how well the conversation goes—the other party has to be on board, too. There might be a person who asks a lot of questions paired with someone who asks none, or a pair where both ask a lot, or a pair where neither do. Each of these dynamics is going to feel different.

The main reason is that each person may share different conversational goals. If both parties have the goal of connecting and getting something done together, the atmosphere will be cooperative. If one or both parties is using the conversation to gain an upper hand, wheedle out information or boast, the interaction becomes competitive. If one or both have very minimal goals for the conversation, it may just fizzle out, and so on.

Understanding that people are coming from different places when they talk to one another helps you in two ways: firstly, you can identify what kind of conversation you're in. If you're stuck with someone hellbent on competition and grandstanding, there may be little you can do but be polite and find a way to exit, or at the least refrain from sharing any information that would put you at a disadvantage. On the other hand, knowing the kind of exchange you *want* to be in can help you actively cerate it with others.

Use follow-up questions. Questions are good, but follow-up questions are better, because they show you were listening, and care enough to keep learning more. Good follow-up questions zone in on an important fact the other person has just shared—if you simply spout off a string of unconnected questions it may feel like an interrogation. But run with what's already been said and you tap into the conversation's momentum and flow.

Use open-ended questions. The idea is that you genuinely want to learn more, so don't go in with a very specific question that puts the other person on the spot or makes it seem like you're only after a particular response. Avoid yes/no questions or leading questions ("So, what do like best about our glorious leader?"). You don't people to feel as though your questions are there simply to extract sensitive information out of you, since this will cause them to clam up or distrust you—rightly!

Use questions to break the ice—gently. It may seem counterintuitive, but if you are curious about something, coming out and asking straight away can help cut through awkwardness faster than beating around the bush. You just have to do it right. No, you don't want to offend people or make them uncomfortable, but a well-pitched question can have an interesting effect— people may feel that you are so curious and interested in their answer that you are willing to gently bend social etiquette. Most people find this flattering! At the very least, you can mask potentially nosy seeming questions with a little humor. Another idea is to proceed your question with a bit of sharing on your part, as though to communicate nonverbally, "I'll show you mine if you show me yours!"

Here's an example of these kinds of questions in action. Picture a quick break room conversation with the new recruit at work. They're a little shy, but you push on and take your chance to start a conversation while you wait for your coffee to brew.

You: "Oh, hi there! You're the new hire in accounting, right?"

Them: "Yup. It's my first day."

You: "Oh, awesome. They're starting you off easy, I hope?" (A gentle question to gauge reaction only.)

Them: "Haha, yeah, I guess. I'm heading to IT right now to get my access code sorted out."

You: "Go on, be honest, what do you think about our state-of-the-art break room? I love working here but me and this microwave do *not* get on." (Breaking the ice, asking emotional/feeling questions rather than dwelling on the facts of what they're up to in the accounting department. Plus, a playful complaint is hard not to respond to.)

Them: "Oh, it's not so bad! You should see mine at home. I think its suicidal, actually."

You: "Ah, great, so you have experience with depressed appliances; you'll fit right in. So, you said you're on your way to IT. Have you met Rob yet?" (Follow-up question.)

Them: "Rob? I don't think so . . ."

You: "Rob's great, you'll love him. I've got to go, but good luck with your microwave! Hey, I should ask, do you live locally? The commute's out here can be hell . . ." (Another follow-up question.)

Them: "Oh yeah, I'm just down the road, in [wherever]."

You: Oh, cool. You should come hang out with some of us on Fridays. We meet up at the bar on the corner . . ."

. . . and so on.

In this conversation, questions are helping everything flow more easily and comfortably. They all seem natural and good-natured, and likely make the new recruit feel respected and paid attention to. In just a two-minute exchange, a great impression is made.

When asking questions, be casual, take your lead from others, and pay attention to group dynamics. Mix up the kinds of questions you ask, but always be mindful about the match between you—are you sharing information, feelings, or values? Respond accordingly, or be prepared to gently try shift the frame with your question.

"Hey, how's it going?" (If said quickly and carelessly, not really a question, just polite conversational protocol—a similarly offhand question or response is probably enough.)

"So you were just released from prison?" (A request for information—possibly more, but this person likely wants to know the precise factual answer.)

"What do you think about the blue? The red looks better doesn't it?" (This is not a request for information—blue or red is irrelevant. The person is unsure which to choose and needs reassurance, or for you to share your own opinion. This is a request for an emotional response.)

"Where do you see our relationship going?" (A request not just for feelings, but broader values, such as whether marriage is important to them. If someone simply responds with how they're feeling right now, it's likely not going to be perceived as a satisfying or complete answer.)

What about when you respond to questions? As we've seen, it's a good idea to be open, and give more information than was asked for. Take your time in answering. Listen for what the person is actually looking for from you—are they just passing the time and being polite, or do they genuinely want to know more? Adjust your answer accordingly.

The Conversational Narcissism Ratio

Have you ever quietly waited for someone to stop speaking, thinking all the while about what you would say the moment they shut up? If so, you've likely been guilty of conversational narcissism! It is the inability to put aside your own internal monologue completely, and focus on what the other person is thinking or saying. It leads to the same outcome of dueling monologues, where conversation hasn't really happened at all—rather, you have two people talking *at* each other instead of *with* each other.

It's also a big reason why people fail to ask questions—or listen properly to their answers.

So, to start with, improve your listening skills by being vigilant about the ways in which craving attention can make you a worse conversationalist. This takes some conscious awareness and also a little honesty. We can ask what our true intentions and motivations are for entering into conversations, in general and specifically with people we know. Are we reaching out to others because we want the validation of their attention? Because we want the feeling of proving ourselves right and another wrong? Because we feel we have to for some reason?

Do we see conversation as a battle, or a game, or a dance? Perhaps we see conversation as an opportunity to show ourselves off, or share what interests us. Whatever your reasons are, though, you probably notice that they usually concern only *you* . . . and don't spare a thought for the other person sharing the conversation with you! How many of us can honestly say that our goal is to see and understand the other person, rather than just to have ourselves seen and understood?

The idea is not to always seek to turn attention to yourself. Conversations should be thought of not as a means to win attention, but to *share* it enjoyably with someone else. The goal is not competition for the floor, but cooperation with an ally. The purpose is to collaborate, not express solely. The aim is to learn, not teach, and so on. For some of us, this may require a complete re-tooling of what we seek when we want to be social.

After an ineffective conversation, people may feel depleted, bored, or even more alone. Good conversations, on the other hand, can be things of beauty, allowing both participants to create between them something bigger than the sum of its parts. One study even discovered that people valued being listened to and heard so much that, in an experiment, were actually willing to pay to enjoy the feeling. That's because that feeling of being acknowledged, heard and respected is incredibly valuable. Offering that feeling to someone else is just as rewarding, if not more so, than experiencing it for yourself. The truth is that if you prioritize the other person in this way, you often end up with a mutually fulfilling conversation anyway, without actually trying.

Listening well requires that you suspend your own self-interest and ego and gracefully allow someone else to shine.

It's now time to get self-conscious and introspective. Sociologist Charles Derber has studied this phenomenon extensively and believes that this form of conversational narcissism can occur without people even being aware it's going on. It can be easy to imagine that conversational narcissists are the stereotypical loudmouths who dominate conversation—but it's far subtler than this. It turns out that the situation can turn on a single word choice. He articulated what he called *support responses* and *shift responses*, and how they can subtly pervade our everyday vocabulary.

Derber explains what he calls "initiatives" in conversation—which can be *attention giving* or *attention seeking*, the latter of which can be further divided into active or passive. This is a little like our tennis analogy—in tennis, we are always either returning the ball or receiving it from the other player, enacting a give and take. In a conversation, what moves back and forth is awareness and attention. These can bounce between people, or pool on one side of the conversation. For our purposes, you can guess which kinds of behaviors we want to orient toward. Let's look at some examples of both in conversation.

Let's first look at support responses, which are what they sound like: words or behaviors that support the expression of the other person in the conversation. For the active, attention-giving variety, a "*support response*" maintains attention on the speaker and their topic—for example, asking a question about what's been said. Support responses can be simple acknowledgements ("Oh really?" "Uh huh."), positively supporting ("That's great!"), or in question form ("What did you say then?"). You can imagine the other person's story is a balloon that everyone else is trying to keep aloft, jumping in here and there to bounce it back up into the air. For instance:

"I love French films."

Response: "Which is your favorite?"

The above response only exists to maintain attention and awareness on the original speaker. The response doesn't interject any new information of its own, but encourages the flow of attention already unfolding. Obviously, this can make people feel, well, supported! This is a great way to validate your conversation partner, let them know you're listening, and send a strong message that you value what they're saying and want to hear more.

The "*shift response,*" however, is an active attention-seeking response that shifts the attention to the other person, in other words back to themselves. It's an act of grabbing the spotlight and pointing it in the opposite direction. With a shift response, the flow of attention and awareness is suddenly diverted elsewhere. What's going on when you see two people vying for attention and talking over one another?

Their dialogue is made exclusively of aggressive shift responses!

"I love French films."

Response: "Yeah? I've never cared much about movies. The other day, actually, I saw this thing at the cinema . . ."

This isn't to say that shift responses are always wrong—in context, they can work, especially if the other person subtly reclaims attention again. Sometimes it might even behoove you to use more shift responses to grab some of the spotlight, or make your feelings known. But how much are you using them?

A shift response is a great idea if you want to move the chat along to another topic, or inject some fresh energy or ideas into the conversation. It's a bad idea if you are simply trying to derail the existing conversation in your favor, so you can say what you want to say. Many people get together and talk this way, each announcing a different personal anecdote that begins with a shift response.

If you have two people with poor listening skills, and both are hell-bent on shift responses, you end up with a wrestling match for attention, rather than a conversation. Maybe both parties are satisfying their lust for expression, but their gas tanks for being heard are running on empty. You may not notice if you are locked in this type of battle, but from the outside looking in, observing this kind of interaction can be curious and confusing.

Moreover, if a bad conversationalist (someone who continually uses shift responses) is paired with a very empathetic listener (someone who continually uses support responses), one party may well feel as though they're having a good talk because the other person is consistently offering them support responses, while that person actually wants to jump off a bridge because the conversation is turning into an awkward pseudo-lecture on the other person's life and beliefs.

What about passive conversational narcissism? Naturally, some people are still quite aware of social norms and etiquette and so will vie for attention in subtler ways. One way of doing this is to fail to offer support responses, waiting till the other person's thread dies away and you can take the limelight. Here, you are hoping that the other person runs out of steam so you can finally get your word in. It is like sitting in a tree and waiting for the prey to get tired and go to sleep—you know it will happen eventually, so you passively bide your time.

Have you been part of a conversation where the other person didn't offer any support responses, even a quaint "Oh really?" or "Uh-huh"? You're not quite sure whether they've taken in what you've said, and that may be intentional on their part. It may have been a case of passive conversational narcissism. It's like letting that balloon drop to the floor. You don't have to do much to make someone else feel that what they're saying hasn't really "landed"!

Most of us are taught that it's polite to not ramble on, to take your turn and then rest, and to share space in conversations. Fine, this person will follow those basic rules. But they sure won't encourage their conversation partner to speak more, lest it cut into their own speaking time! A lack of (genuine!) feedback from the other person can quickly make someone feel they ought to stop speaking—and this is where the conversational narcissist steps back into the picture.

Though it's tempting to try to catch other people in the act of conversational narcissism, its far more productive to learn to notice it in *yourself* and guard against it. You can't control what others do, but you can control your actions and how good of a listener you are. After all, that is the goal of this book. For the other purpose, you may want to seek a book on persuasion or hypnosis.

The irony is it's often those who are able to listen well, to step aside, and to take a genuine interest in their conversation partners who become people we think of as most interesting, charismatic and worthy of our attention in the first place. So the purported goal of conversational narcissism (*making darn sure that people know things about you*) isn't even satisfied. Oops. Luckily, there are a few guidelines to battle these unconscious obstacles you'll undoubtedly face.

Balance your needs and desires with other people's.

To do this, you first need to be aware of your focus and where it's going. Pay attention to how the airtime is being distributed. Is one person doing all the talking? Is there a back-and-forth? This requires more than just playing at being interested in another person's life—you genuinely need to forget yourself for a moment and engage fully, and honestly, in what someone else is saying. Stop thinking about your response for the future, and pay attention to what someone is currently saying to you.

This means no rushing in to explain or frame what they've said so that it relates back to you again. Give more supportive responses, and guard against constantly referring every topic back to yourself. Ask questions to invite the other person to say more. If you take attention for a while, enjoy it—but volley it back again. Like we were taught as children: It's good to share!

"As you were talking, it made me think about this experience I had once, where XYZ. That made me wonder, did you find that XYZ was the case as well?" A person saying this demonstrates that they're willing to share the conversation, rather than hog it all for themselves.

Think about ego, power, self-esteem, and control.

Those who seem most boastful in a conversation, who jealously guard attention or speak over others, are often those who feel most insecure in themselves. Their need to control the conversation comes from a hunger for attention and approval. If you find yourself using conversations as a platform to boost your ego, feel better about yourself, or be witnessed and supported by others, your work may be to learn to be comfortable taking the back seat for a change. The paradox is that people who seem most likeable and confident are those who don't appear to be making frantic efforts to dominate others' attention.

What Would Conan Do and Curiosity

Let's return to an idea we touched on earlier—the idea of playfulness and curiosity in conversation. Curiosity plays a huge role in the way we receive others and thus how they receive us. You can be the most charming, funniest person in the room, but if you aren't *interested and curious* about the person across from you, there simply won't be a connection. Why would there be? It's more like a one-man show than a conversation. Big surprise, it turns out that we care if the person across from us is engaged or scanning the room behind us and looking for someone better to talk to.

Staying curious is a difficult proposition because, at first glance, most people might seem uninteresting or unworthy of paying attention to. This is harsh, but it is in fact behind a lot of people's reason for "hating small talk." This is undoubtedly the biggest hurdle for most of us—even if you don't consciously think it, you subconsciously believe that someone is simply not worth being curious about. You think that even if you dig deeper you won't find anything worth your time, so why bother in the first place?

It's true that, at first glance, very few of us are compelling. You included. But acting on this impulse will limit your communication and keep you right where you are. We are cutting off people's *ability* to be interesting

139

and compelling because we don't give them a chance. In the end, it doesn't particularly matter what you believe. Just start to build the habit of curiosity, and eventually it won't matter if you think people are worthy or not (they are). You'll be able to find the interesting aspects in just about anyone, and that's what counts.

To do so, I've found that the absolute best mindset to emulate is that of a talk show host—Jimmy Fallon, Jimmy Kimmel, Conan O'Brien, whoever your favorite is, they all do the same thing. Just ask yourself what they would do if you're struggling for what curiosity looks like and how you can wield it. Conan O'Brien happens to my favorite, so let's think about the traits he embodies in a conversation with a guest on his show.

Visualize his studio. He's got a big open space, and he is seated at a desk. His guest is seated at a chair adjacent to the desk, and it's literally like they exist in a world of their own. When Conan has a guest on his show, that guest is the center of his world for the next ten minutes. They are the most interesting person he has ever come across, everything they say is spellbinding, he is insatiably curious about their stories, and he reacts to anything they say with an uproarious laugh and an otherwise exaggerated reaction that they were seeking. He is charmingly positive and can always find a humorous spin on a negative aspect of a story.

His sole purpose is to make his guest comfortable on the show, encourage them to talk about themselves, and ultimately make them feel good and look good. In turn, this makes them share revealing things they might not otherwise share and create a connection and chemistry with him that is so important for a talk show. The viewers at home are desperate to learn about this celebrity guest, so Conan acts as a proxy for their curiosity. Also, the viewers can tell in an instant if either party is mailing it in or faking it, so Conan's job literally depends on his ability to use his curiosity to connect on a deeper level.

Even with grumpy or more quiet guests, he is able to elevate their energy levels and attitudes simply by being intensely interested in them (at an energy level slightly above theirs) and encouraging them by giving them the great reactions that they seek. It's almost as if he plays the game "How little can I say to get the most out of people?" It's a non-obvious talent that is worth its weight in gold—and it'll make the person receive this attention feel like solid gold!

Of course, in your life, you may be faced with those people that are like pulling teeth to talk to. A little bit of friendly encouragement and affirmation can make even the meekest clam open up. Numerous questions, directing the conversation toward them, and the feeling that you actually care are also integral. Imagine the relief you can create at dreaded networking events. People like those who like them, so when you react the way they want, it encourages them to be more outgoing and open with you.

Other talk show hosts would later go on the record lamenting how often they disliked his guests and how boring he found the actors and actresses that he would be forced to speak to. But the fact that this is never really detected is a testament to how highly trained his habit of curiosity was. He started by making a conscious decision to be curious, built the habit, and engaged his guests easily; do you think his guests could tell if he was interested or not? Never.

Curiosity allows people to feel comfortable enough to speak freely beyond a superficial level—because you are demonstrating that you care and that you will listen when they open up. People won't be inclined to reveal their secret thoughts if they think it will be met with apathy, after all. So whether you have to fake it till you make it, Conan O'Brien is who your mindset and attitude should feel like.

It's a banal and often-used quote, but for good reason. Dale Carnegie said it best: "You can make more friends in two months by becoming truly interested in other people than you can in two years by trying to get other people interested in you."

In case Conan O'Brien's curiosity still isn't coming naturally to you, here are some more specific patterns of thought you can use to improve your people skills.

I wonder what they are like? When you start to wonder about the other person, it changes your perspective on them completely. This is an inkling of curiosity. You start to care about them—not only about their shallow traits, such as their occupation or how their day is going, but what motivates them and what makes them act in the way they do.

Having a sense of wonder about someone is one of the most powerful mindsets you can have because it makes you want to scratch your itch. Scratching the itch of curiosity will become secondary to everything else because you simply want to know about the other person. Here, you don't have to *like* them, exactly—it goes deeper than that. Just perceive them, as much of them as you possibly can, and genuinely allow yourself to be amazed by that.

Suppose you had a sense of wonder about computers as a child. You were probably irritating with how many questions you asked anyone that seemed to have knowledge about computers. What kind of attention span are you going to devote to computers, and what kind of questions are you going to ask? You are going to skip the small talk interview questions and get right down to the details because it's what you care and wonder about.

Keeping the mindset of wonderment will completely change the way you interact with people because you will suddenly care, and much of the time, we don't notice that we don't care about the person we are talking to. You'll dig deeper and deeper until you can put together a picture of what you are wondering about.

It's important to note here that you need to be sincere about it. Conan is a pro who gets a salary from the job he does, but for the rest of us, it's so much better to foster a genuine interest in others rather than fake it. That boring person you're chatting to? Challenge yourself and your assumptions about them. They have a history, secrets, hopes, dreams, unexpected talents—what are they?

What can they teach me? Don't read this from the perspective of attempting to gain what you can from someone. Read it from the perspective of seeing others as being people worthy of your attention. Everyone has valuable knowledge, whether it applies to your life or not. Everyone is great at something, and everyone is a domain expert in something that you are not, no matter how small or obscure. People's perspectives have innate value, and just by learning about them, we are enriched.

The main point is to ignite an interest in the other person as opposed to an apathetic approach. Imagine if you were a huge skiing junkie and you met someone that used to be a professional skier. They may have even reached the Olympics in their prime.

What will follow? You'll be thrilled by what you can potentially learn and gain from the other person, and that will guide the entire interaction. Again, there will be a level of interest and engagement if you view others as worthy of talking to. But you'd never know unless you dug.

Whether we like to admit it or not, sometimes we feel some people are not worth our time. It's a bad habit, and this line of thinking is one of the first steps toward breaking it. *Everyone* is worth our time, but you won't be able to discover it if you don't put in the work. At the very least, most people have had interesting or noteworthy experiences in life. Become curious and you just may find that your grandma's Bungo friend was an exotic dancer during the war, that the friend you knew for twenty years has a secret passion for vintage magazines, and your work colleague actually used to be a missionary in the Congo before she had kids. Who knew!

What do we have in common? This is an investigation into the life experiences you share with someone. It instantly makes them more engaging and interesting— because we feel that they are more similar to us! It may sound a bit egotistical, but we are undoubtedly more captivated by people that share the same views and interests as us, and they us.

It may even *elevate* people, especially if we are surrounded by people different from us. For instance, if you discovered that a new stranger was born in the same hospital as you were, despite being in a different country, you would instantly feel more open to them. This person *must* share similar worldviews, values, and humor. You now have a positive bias toward them, actively seeking out more good in them. But you wouldn't have discovered that if you didn't make an attempt at digging.

You are going to be on a hunt, and you will ask the important questions that get you where you want to be. You might jump from topic to topic, or you might dive in and ask directly.

Perhaps it's just because you will have something to fixate on besides talking for talking's sake, but these attitudes will drastically change how you approach people. Curiosity can still be hard, which is why my final suggestion for creating curiosity is to make a game of it. Your goal is to learn as much about the other person as possible. Alternatively, assume there is something extremely thrilling and exciting about the other person and make it your quest to find it. Eventually, you'll find what you're looking for.

The next time you go out to a café or store, put these attitudes to the test with the captive audience of the baristas or cashiers you come across—the lucky few who are paid to be nice to you. Do you perceive these workers to be below you, or do you treat them differently than you would treat a good friend? Do you have a sense of wonderment and curiosity about them? What do you think they can teach you, and what do you have in common with them?

Do you tend to ask the baristas or cashiers about their day and actually care about their answer? If not, do you think you'll be able to simply "turn it on" when you're around people you care about? Practice your mindsets about the people around you. It's the easiest practice you'll have because you don't have to lift a finger, but it drastically transforms the quality of relationships you'll create.

Takeaways

- In order to interact and engage more fully in conversations, we need to work against our not-so-useful habits and learn better ones.
- A non-negotiable habit is becoming a master at using questions. The right questions help people feel closer to us, communicate our attention and care, share our competence, show that we're aware and paying attention, deepen

intimacy, guide the conversation, and make us more trustworthy.

- All exchanges, and hence all questions, are typically on one of three possible levels: those exchanging factual information, those exchanging feelings and emotions, and those communicating deeper values. In social situations, you'll lean more heavily on the last two, but a good conversation works when people have similar conversational goals and are matched in the level they're interacting on.

- Conversational narcissism is an impediment to curiosity, engagement, and good question asking. Whether unconscious or conscious, this usually results from us placing something other than connection with the other person as our goal for conversation, i.e. to brag, to defend, to compete.

- We can reduce our own conversational narcissism by using questions. Follow-up questions are very effective, as are open-ended questions that don't make people uncomfortable, but may *gently* push on the barrier or normal etiquette.

- Just as a role model can be a guide and inspiration for your own behavior, a model can also help you stay curious when you talk to others. Talk show hosts are experts and placing their conversation partners front and center, so we can ask, what would they do? Usually, the answer is "treat my guest like the most interesting person in the whole universe."

- Curiosity needs to be genuine. We all have a bias against others sometimes, assuming they're not very interesting, but unless we ask, we won't learn about their more fascinating sides. Assume that everyone has something to teach you, and foster a genuine inquisitiveness into the details of their world. I guarantee you will not be disappointed.

Chapter 5. Engagement

In this chapter, we're going to be looking firstly at *how* to engage with people in conversations, and secondly *what* to engage on. You've seen how important it is to get your own mindset sorted, to practice sharing, asking questions, and to avoid all those obstacles that get in the way of genuine connection.

In reading the previous chapters, you might have assumed that human interaction boils down to light-hearted chat at the water cooler or lively conversations at the club. But what do you do when a co-worker bursts into tears at her desk? How do you react when your newly made friend confesses that they're actually battling alcoholism? Real life isn't all pick-up lines and banter—occasionally, small talk will include engaging with people on negative or difficult topics. This is why we'll look at another important concept for anyone that wants to get a real handle on small talk: validation.

Validation

Validation is a kind of communication, and its purpose is to communicate **acceptance**.

If you're nervous, introverted or just out of practice when it comes to socializing, the main thing in your mind is probably how to get others to accept you. But, learning to convey acceptance of other people is an important part of the puzzle, too—perhaps a bigger part. Validation means that we perceive and acknowledge someone for who they are.

Let's take a look now at a step-by-step, detailed framework to follow when we want to provide validation. In reality, the six levels described above flow and blend into one another. There are different techniques, approaches and skills associated with each that, again, will vary in their effectiveness depending on the person you're talking to. Let's consider each in finer detail.

The examples we'll consider now lean more toward supporting people and being a kind ear, but they apply to any and all situations—it's just a matter of degree. Validation is something that's most useful for those times when our conversation partners are feeling vulnerable, upset or emotional in some way. You might not have considered responding to this kind of thing as part of "small talk," but the fact is that learning to engage compassionately with people who are distressed and being a dazzling and witty conversationalist are one and the same skill.

Step 1 – How to be Present: Listen!

Yes, we're harping on listening skills just one more time. No matter what the situation is, you should always go into it with an open mind and calm, focused attention on the other person. You are not coming in with an agenda. Rather, you are listening carefully to better understand their point of view, and their experience.

This can actually be the hardest part, because when we have a goal in mind of how the conversation is "supposed" to go, we may want to jump in and start talking, tell stories, and so on.

But resist this urge in the beginning and let the other person take the lead. Let them speak and really listen. Here, your verbal communication is turned off for the most part, but your non-verbal communication comes to the fore.

Receptive body language: maintain an open posture and facial expression and turn your body to face them. Relax. Make eye contact if it feels appropriate, but it's eye contact that is about interested, respectful attention rather than interrogation. Mirror their body language as closely as you can. If they're sitting with their legs crossed, do the same. If they have their arms resting on a table, you should too. Get rid of distractions—put your phone away, turn the TV off and show, with your body, "I'm here now, and I want to listen to what you have to say." It's also a good idea to match their tone and pace of speaking, as well as their "energy." If they are quiet and hesitant, for example, be quiet too, and tread carefully.

You might also encourage them to open up by asking, "Go on, tell me what you *really* think, I'm all ears." You might make encouraging "uh-huh" sounds or something similar, but at this step, silence can work wonders as an invitation for the other person to share.

Examples: Your roommate has just come home and clearly seems shaken up. Seeing this, you close your laptop and turn toward him, showing a concerned expression. He says he's just had a car accident and is feeling pretty stunned. Without saying too much (maybe a simple, "Tell me what happened."), you sit next to him and just listen without interrupting as he tells his story.

Or, imagine a woman tells her husband they need to talk. They sit down to chat, and she begins to explain something that's been bothering her, and that she's upset with him. Though it's tempting for the husband to respond immediately to what feels like accusations, he waits until she's said her piece.

Although he doesn't really like what he's hearing, he tries hard to just listen, and see things from her point of view, even though he would really like to share his own. When she's done talking, he pauses a little, so she doesn't feel as though he was simply waiting for her to shut up so he could jump in with a rebuttal!

For a more casual small talk example, there are little things you can do that say a lot: make a show of putting away your phone and turning to focus all your attention on the person in front of you. Lean in. After they say something, pause to show you're really mulling it over, and whatever you do, don't interrupt!

Step 2 – How to Reflect: Ask Questions

If the person simply wanted to be heard, and immediately feels better, you can sometimes stop at step 1. But you may find the conversation naturally shifts to your response to what you've heard. This is actively letting someone know you've heard them, because when you paraphrase what they've said, you are reflecting it back to them.

But when you reflect back, it only feels validating if it's *accurate*. The easiest way to do this is to literally repeat what you've heard. You can use reflection to summarize what's been said, to reiterate the most important parts of the story, or to distill some main essence of what they're feeling. For example, if somebody blurts out a long list of stressful events that have happened to them that day, you can say "Wow, it seems like there's so much going on right now."

Don't worry about your statement seeming overly obvious. When you reflect back, it's as though you are helping the other person tell their story. It lets them know that you're listening, and that you *get* it. It tells them that what they're expressing has actually landed, and communication is working.

Now, you don't have to jump in with clever-sounding guesses or tell them what they're feeling—if you don't know, you can always ask! Asking questions is further confirmation that you're listening and invested, and that what they say matters. Questions can prompt a person to keep sharing and help them arrive at a more distinct conclusion themselves, in their own time.

Supportive questions:

"Okay, I want to understand what you mean when you say XYZ . . . can you tell me more?"

"So what did you think about that?"

"What do you think happens next?"

"Can you say more about XYZ?"

"So how are you feeling about all of this?"

Though it's not a bad question per se, avoid, "So how does that make you feel?" as it can obviously feel a little cheesy!

Examples: If someone has just explained at length a complicated family drama, you may be a little confused on the details. Asking questions can show that you care about grasping the subtleties. "So, what's the relationship like between your mother and sister?" or "So you're worried that they had that discussion without you? Have I got that right?" Outright asking if you've understood correctly not only shows that you want to understand, but that you are centering the other person, which is validating in itself.

Questions are not just for your own clarification, though. You might well know how a particular story ends, but asking questions about it communicates encouragement and acceptance of the other person working their way through the story. "Okay, so then your mom told you about this conversation with your sister. What happened next?"

Questions and statements can both be used to achieve the same effect. Whether you frame it as an obvious question or more of a tentative statement, you are essentially asking, *Have I understood? Is this how it is for you?*

No, not every casual conversation is going to resemble a therapy session, but in a way, the skills practiced in each are not dissimilar. At the very least, stopping to reflect back what you're being told buys you some time—it's easier than asking questions because you're literally just conforming what you've been told, and essentially prompting the other person to keep going with their story.

Step 3 – How to mindread: Use feeling words

If you spend a while in the previous step, you may find yourself naturally flowing into this step, where you speak more directly about the other person's experience. You began by listening and helping the person tell their story, and as you continue, it's as though you are helping them add more shape and structure to it. This makes sense when you think about it: when people are sharing something on an emotional level, they may not be thinking super clearly or rationally. Remember, the purpose of this kind of conversation is *not* to transmit factual information. They need to first express the emotions they're feeling, and only then find their way to processing and integrating the experience.

At this early stage though, try to avoid injecting your own interpretations into things. Think of yourself as a kind of guide or even midwife, helping a person get through their own experience, without making it too much about yourself. Sometimes, when people are upset, it can be helpful to put words to what they're feeling. Simply being able to say, "I'm feeling so disappointed right now," is a step toward acknowledging and owning your own experience.

"Mindreading" is perhaps a misleading word here, since you shouldn't really feel like you are guessing. But *tentatively* offer up an emotion word that might capture what they're going through. In doing so, you are helping people arrive at their own interpretations and conclusions. Naturally, you shouldn't just blurt out, "You're depressed" or flat-out tell someone how they're feeling.

Phrases to try:

"It seems to me like . . ."

"I'm wondering if XYZ is the case . . ."

"You seem quite irritated/happy/nervous/confused right now." (Said in a totally non-judgmental tone.)

"Do you think that made you feel XYZ?"

"I can see why you feel that way. So would I!"

"From what you're saying, it sounds like you're feeling XYZ about the whole thing."

"That's understandable!"

Examples: Someone might be explaining at length the irritating things one of their friends does, giving a list of offenses, including the most recent one that caused a small argument. But in listening to them, you notice that they haven't actually stated outright how they feel. It might be obvious to you both, but you say, "Woah, seems like there's definitely a lot of frustration in this friendship."

By putting a single word to the collection of experiences, you not only show that you've listened, but that you can actually synthesize everything together, and see the bigger picture. This can really move a conversation along, and the other person might say, "Yes, that's exactly right. We seem to get *frustrated* with each other more and more lately . . ."

Though it's never your job to tell someone how they're feeling, they may get to see their emotions a lot more clearly when you reflect them back. If a different friend is complaining about how they're fed up with their girlfriend's male friends, you might say after a while, "I wonder if it's jealousy you're feeling?" If you get really good at this skill, it will start to seem like magic to people. Sadly, many people out there are so used to not being heard that when someone simply does listen and reflects back their emotions to them, they can feel enormous validation. It's no superpower, though—you've just shown them that you're listening!

Even if you get the mindreading part wrong, so long as you're not being madly offensive, the other person is likely to appreciate the effort, and in correcting you, they are again engaged in sharing openly—a win-win situation.

Step 4 – How to Find Context: Validate and Center Their Experience

Again, one step may bleed over into the next, and asking questions or mindreading may easily lead to this step. At this stage, you want to communicate a strong sense of understanding who the person is, and how their experience is truly unique to them. You want to center them and focus on their world and how it feels to be in it.

Here, you are still not offering your own interpretations, but rather helping the other person draw together their ideas so that they find their own conclusions themselves. We can absolutely provide validation to people we don't know that well, but more commonly, we know a little about them and their history.

When we validate and center another person, we are saying to them *your perspective is valid. This story and the way you're experiencing it makes sense.* For example, we can say, "I can totally see why you freaked out when that happened. Seeing as you've had bad experiences with this sort of thing in the past, it's not surprising you reacted the way you did."

We can bring in plenty of validation by acknowledging a person's unique perspective and history. This can make people feel really seen and heard. This is such a rare commodity in our world today, that if you can respond this way to someone in their hour of need, you can consider them a friend from then on. Some of the following phrases can be used alone to provide validation but can also be extended and framed in terms of the person's context, or the broader situation.

Phrases that Validate a Person's Unique Experience:

"I can really see how the situation has made you feel this way."

"Given that you're a woman/Muslim/Australian/gymnast, I can understand why you responded as you did."

"What you say makes total sense to me."

"It's understandable that you feel like this."

"Well, you have a reason for feeling the way you do, and I completely understand that."

Example: If someone tells you they are struggling with PTSD after experiencing a violent crime, you can start by listening (being present), then ask them questions to flesh out their experience of the anxiety (so you can reflect). Then you might move on to saying something that vaguely summarizes their experience (mindreading, for example, "You've been under so much stress, I'm sure.") and extend this by embedding it into the bigger context ("Given what you've already been through, it's no surprise that you feel like this.").

If on the other hand someone's been dumped or their ice cream has fallen on the floor, you can use *exactly* the same skill set, only dialed back slightly.

Step 5 – How to Normalize: Refrain from Judgment

Judgment and acceptance cannot exist at the same time. When we validate people, we acknowledge that their experience is valid and their own, whatever it is. We can't do this properly if we have loads of criticisms or judgments about what we think of them. Maybe we don't agree with their appraisal of events. Maybe we think they're being foolish or missing something important. Maybe they're angry with us, and we want to defend ourselves. Or maybe we can't quite understand their response and it really does seem irrational to us.

Nevertheless, when we seek to normalize someone's experience, what we are really doing is telling them that it is *acceptable*, and that we don't judge them for what they're going through. You don't have to agree or share their opinion. You don't have to relate to the way they're telling their story or what they're choosing to focus on. As we've seen, that belongs more to an informational exchange conversation—which is not what you are in. But you can still communicate that *they* are entitled to feel the way they do, regardless of how your experience compares to theirs.

Many people have had the experience of reaching out to others for support, sympathy or (let's face it) a good old-fashioned rant, only to have their experience judged. They want to feel validated and heard, but instead, the other person might launch into a fact-finding mission, trying to root out who's to blame, and why, and what the logical and "correct" answer is.

Alternatively, some people may see the emotions of others as quite threatening, awkward or uncomfortable. Because they feel unable to validate and accept, for example, sad feelings in themselves, they react badly when they see them in others. Their response then is to judge. "Oh, you're overreacting. It's not that bad," or "Come on now, you're being a bummer. Cheer up!" An even worse outcome is someone who almost relishes the other's vulnerability and seems to get a kick out of their misfortune ("I told you so!").

When we normalize, however, we communicate that all feelings and all experiences are valid. Just because some feelings are uncomfortable or confronting, it doesn't mean that people are wrong for experiencing them. The other side of the coin, though, is that we can also be guilty of judging in the opposite direction, especially if we are trying to be supportive or helpful. When we say something like, "Oh, it's so healthy that you're finally grieving that loss," or "You go girl, get mad!" we are also passing a value judgment on an experience.

We need to look beyond the specific emotion, thought or experience and to the person having it. We need to be able to say to that person: "It's okay to be who you are right now and feel how you feel." Deep down, don't all of us want to know that we are not bad or wrong or strange? Don't we all feel a little better when we know that we're not the only people who feel the way we do?

Ways to Express Non-Judgment and Normalize:

"I think that most people would feel that way if they were in your shoes."

"It's totally normal that you feel like this."

"I would be upset too."

"There's nothing wrong with thinking these thoughts."

"You're not alone."

"Hey, I'm glad you told me how you feel." (Normalizing the act of sharing.)

Sometimes, the best way to show our acceptance and convey a sense of normalcy is not in the words we say, but in how we act, and what we *don't* say. Try to avoid making a pronouncement on what thoughts and feelings are good or bad. Don't comment on the strength or appropriateness of the feeling, for example, by suggesting an emotion is too much or too little.

If you take the time to think about it, genuinely likable people are often the most accepting and non-judgmental. Somehow, they seem secure and confident in themselves because they accept others for who they are. This is not so far removed from the idea of play we discussed earlier—it comes down to simply being in the moment with the person as they are, without getting bogged down in what things "should" be.

Examples: A child reveals a rather shocking secret to their mother, but the mother is careful not to act horrified. By saying, "I'm glad I know, you were right to tell me, and it's understandable that you're upset about this," she communicates both that the child's feelings are valid, and also that reaching out and sharing is welcome and acceptable—a profoundly reassuring position to take when someone is in distress.

Normalizing can be done briefly and as a matter of course, too. For example, someone shares something with their therapist and finishes with, "But I'm sure you're used to seeing way more important problems in your practice." The therapist can respond, "Your problem *is* important. And many people come here with the very same concerns as you."

One thing you might not have thought about is how you communicate absence (or fail to) in the way you talk about *yourself*. If you have confidence and a robust sense of your own worth, and act that way, others can pick up on it and trust you more to bring the same equanimity and compassion to them. If on the other hand you're self-critical, others might rightly wonder if you'll be that way with them.

Step 6 – How to Show Genuine Validation: Be Real

When someone reaches out for help and support, the last thing they want is to feel like doing so makes them weak or wrong. Remember that vulnerability actually takes courage, and facing it helps us get closer to one another, not further. When opening up to others, we all like to imagine that they understand a little about what we're saying, because they're human too, and have experienced suffering, loss, confusion, and other negative feelings. When the person listening can open up a little in return, we can feel immensely validated. We are not just being *told* we are okay and not alone—we actually experience it for real.

This final step of showing genuine human care and understanding is something that can't be faked. But one way to do it is to offer up something of your own experience. This isn't to derail the conversation or hog attention, but to confirm that you, too, know a little of what it feels like. "I lost my father last year, and I remember feeling that way, too."

Yes, it's always better to listen more and talk less, and you don't want to succumb to a preachy bit of advice or a story about how you did things better, but being a little vulnerable yourself can be a powerful thing to do. Don't share a story just to make a point or sneak in some advice—for example, "When my father died, I took up jogging. It was the only thing that kept me sane," (i.e. I think *you* should do the same). Rather, you are showing them that you are familiar with their emotion on a firsthand level.

We won't look at helpful phrases or examples here since the point of this step is to react genuinely, as the real person you are. Be honest. It can be as simple as saying "I know how you feel," but, if you can truly *show* that you know, even better. "Did I ever tell you that the same thing happened to me last year?" And if you can't relate, it's probably better to just say that you can't, instead of trying to shoehorn your own experience in an attempt to match theirs.

As you can see, at no point in this process are you fixing any problems, offering any solutions, advice or suggestions, arguing, blaming, figuring out "the truth" or deciding whether the person's reactions are reasonable or not. You're also not trying to "help" by giving sagely words of wisdom or using your own experience as an inspiring example.

The above process may take an hour to unfold, with several loops back to previous stages. The person may need to dig deeper, rehash some things or tell the tale again before they're ready to move on or even ask for advice. Or, the process may be over in a minute, and not proceed all the way through. The way validation unfolds depends on just two things:

- The needs of the person receiving the validation

- The capacities, limits and skill of the person giving the validation

If you feel like a total amateur at the art of communication, then the above may seem like diving in at the deep end—surely you should just start with some easy ice breakers and some tips on how to be witty? The thing is, the whole separation between small and big talk is not really there in real life—*all* talk matters, if it's aim is about people trying to connect, whether that's in big ways or small. So many people try so hard to impress others, to convince them of how great they are, to appear invincible. The ironic thing is how often this has no effect at all, compared to simply being present, genuine, kind, and accepting. If you can practice this—with yourself and others—you may find that there are far fewer barriers to connection than you once thought.

HPM

Okay, so validation is important. Genuine compassion, listening, and all that jazz are great. Got it. But by now you're probably still wondering about . . . the actual words you say. What to literally fill those uncomfortable silences with when they crop up. It's taken us to chapter 5 to get here, but that's because simply parroting rote phrases or lines without understanding why or how to do it properly will get you nowhere. But now that you've laid the groundwork, we can get into the nitty gritty. *What should you say?*

Something that tends to create awkward silence is when people run out of things to talk about. It happens. Of course, the problem isn't that people are so boring or uninformed that they literally have nothing to say on a matter or topic. It's usually a problem of not feeling comfortable enough to say what's on their mind, and thus they can't think of anything to say that they feel is properly filtered. Once self-censorship, doubt, anxiety, second-guessing, and apathy kick in, a conversation can seriously stall and sputter out.

Here, I want to introduce six extremely effective types of responses for just about anything. This is important because, as you know, our minds go blank sometimes. This is not because you're boring or the other person is. It's not because you're not prepared enough or have low confidence.

And it's not because you're not being validating or accepting enough. It just happens! But we can work around it. Having these six types of responses means you can literally go down the list until you find something useful—and there will be.

HPM

HPM is one of my favorite conversation tactics because I believe it is so widely applicable.

It stands for History, Philosophy, and Metaphor.

History is not the subject history as in the ancient Egyptians or World War II, but your personal experience and memories about the topic at hand. Everyone has memories, even if they have to borrow the memories of other people. To tap into this stream of ideas, imagine the key phrase as *I remember when I . . .*

Philosophy is again not the subject, but your personal feelings, stance, or opinion on the topic at hand. Everyone has personal feelings, again, even if they have to borrow from someone else. Imagine the key phrase as *I really love/hate that because . . .*

Finally, Metaphor is an external topic, related or not, that the topic at hand reminds you of. It's about finding links and connections that pull things together. Everyone can create metaphors; it's just a matter of practicing your sense of imagination. Imagine the key phrase as *That totally makes me think of . . .*

The very point of HPM is that everyone has an H, P, and M. The reason I feel it is widely applicable is because everyone has these things in their life. They are always accessible to you. You have memories, you have opinions, and you likely can make connections if you bother to think about them—so knowing about HPM is almost like having cue cards right in front of you while you are immersed in a conversation or stuck in an awkward silence.

All you need to do is think HPM when you're faced with a pending silence or awkward moment and you'll have something to say.

There will always be uncomfortable spots in any conversation. It doesn't matter if you're the best conversationalist in the world. There will always be those times when conversation dwindles away or there is dead air. By knowing HPM, you increase the likelihood that awkward spots won't be noticeable at all.

Let's put HPM into action with a topic you feel you have nothing to say about. For me, this would be something like NASCAR (car racing). After all, I live in San Francisco, and the mediocre public transportation system is what the vast majority of people use to get around here.

Suppose someone brings up their love of NASCAR, which I know almost nothing about. My HPM would go like this:

History: I've never been to a NASCAR event, but they look incredible. One of my friends said it was unexpectedly thrilling. Have you been to many? [My lack of personal history and drawing on someone else's history regarding NASCAR—great! And excuse to ask questions and show my interest]

Philosophy: NASCAR events look amazingly fun. I feel that it's something you have to be in the stadium for. It's got to be more than just sitting and watching the cars, right? (Asserting an opinion about

NASCAR events. Sure, you could try listing all the reasons you hate the idea of NASCAR racing, and you'd certainly get a conversation going . . . but it might not exactly be the conversation you want!)

Metaphor: Those NASCAR cars always have lots of sponsors, right? Reminds me of European soccer teams and their uniforms. Crazy! (Took an element of the topic and related it to something entirely different.)

Let's try it with another topic so you get the hang of it a bit better. In real life conversations, things might come up completely randomly, so in that spirit I'll do the same and suggest something out-there: dinosaurs. Someone brings up their love of dinosaurs upon seeing a picture of one on a movie poster.

History: My favorite movie of all time is actually *Jurassic Park*, so me too. I remember the first time I watched it. I couldn't sleep for a few days.

Philosophy: I love dinosaurs, too. My favorite is the triceratops; they always seemed so sweet. Which is yours?

Metaphor: Dinosaurs remind me of our friend Jim. They have the same body structure, right?

It's a simple example, but you get the idea. The wonderful thing is that you don't have to work very hard to think about your own past, your opinions, or random connections between things. If you're floundering, just reach for your HPM like a life jacket and you'll get the conversation moving again.

But while HPM is great, it doesn't resonate with everyone. There are a couple of aspects to note. First, it's all about you. This can be good or bad. If you feel you need to share more about yourself, then it's great. However, if you find that you constantly insert your own stories into the conversation, it's not so great. To counter this, you could make sure that you're ending any anecdote with a question that volleys attention back to the other person. (Like we did above—simply ask, "What about you?" to show you aren't hogging the conversation.)

Second, HPM requires you to draw internally and determine what you think about something, or access something from your memory banks. It can be difficult to generate original thoughts and statements without practice, and can take many of us out of the moment completely. HPM is completely user-generated, instead of building upon something else from the conversation. Luckily for you, you've already got some practice with your "conversational resume" from an earlier chapter. In fact, these two ideas can be woven together—use HPM as a quick reminder of certain ideas, and then flesh them out with material from your conversational resume.

If HPM is not workable though, for whatever reason, there is another three-letter acronym here to help you out. SBR is really useful but the complete opposite of HPM: while HPM draws on material internally, SBR draws on it externally.

SBR

SBR stands for Specific, Broad, and Related. This means you work with the exact topic that is given, and make statements or ask questions about it in a specific, broad, or related manner. Easy! For many people, this is simpler because it allows them to just work in the moment and react to the last thing that was said to them—not to mention you don't necessarily have to bring yourself into it, so it's more appropriate for things like work conversations. You can also be more of a parrot when you use SBR (a charming, witty parrot, obviously).

SBR is a great conversation device because it's contextual. It doesn't require reaching into your memory banks or expertise the way HPM does. There's nothing to learn or memorize, except the acronym. SBR sticks to the topics that you're already talking about and manipulates or repositions them so you can remain on topic. In some cases, you may have hit a point in the conversation where HPM is unavailable or just doesn't make sense for you. In those cases, you can quickly snap into SBR.

Here's how SBR works.

S stands for Specific. This is when you ask a question or make a statement that goes deeper and more in-depth about the topic at hand.

For example, if someone is talking about building cars, you might ask questions like,

"So then what happens when you build it this way?" or "I've never heard of someone doing that. How long does that take exactly, and what tools do you need?"

Even if you don't know anything about the topic, and sometimes especially when you don't know anything about the topic, bounce it back to the person speaking so you can learn more. Give the other person the spotlight and allow them to get into the nitty gritty details. Ask for them. When you get specific, you also inevitably touch upon people's thought processes and motivations, something people typically love to share. Remember, you don't have to rescue the conversation all on your own— there are other people.

If they are building something, try to find out how it works and why they are doing it. Try to gain enough knowledge such that you could build it yourself at some point. Act as if you are really trying to gain a deep understanding of what is happening in the topic. You can combine this with everything learnt from the question asking section earlier, or use this as an opportunity to simultaneously reflect that you have in fact been listening and paying attention.

Why questions are good here. *Who, what, when,* and *where* questions work better in the next category.

B stands for Broad. This is when you ask a question or make a statement that is more general to the topic at hand. Where before you zoomed in, here you are zooming out.

As mentioned, if someone is telling you about how they are building a car, you can ask *who, what, when,* and *where* questions. Who did you build it with? What kind of car was it? When was this? Where did you keep the parts?

Broad questions take a step back and collect the context and background of a topic, which might be necessary to being able to understand the topic at all. You aren't necessarily changing topics, but you are seeing what topics are interrelated with the one you are zooming away from. If someone tells you about their ski trip, zooming out would be to discover the context of the trip, where they went, whom they went with, and what happened. You are trying to understand the topic from a bird's eye view. Naturally, this kind of thing fits well in the start of a conversation, and helps get things going.

R stands for Related. If you can't think of anything specific or broad to say, you can find a topic related to the topic at hand. This is similar to the metaphor portion of HPM because the questions are somewhat alike. Remember the key phrase there—*That makes me think of . . .*

For example, if the topic at hand is building cars, you don't need to ask more about it if you flat out don't care. Sure, you're not interested in cars. But that doesn't mean you're not interested in the other person, or in the conversation more generally. Just take a tiny element, however related or unrelated, and use it to bring up a different topic. Use it as a springboard or launching pad.

Building cars makes me think of the gym . . . It's such hard work, right?

Building cars reminds me of building my computer. Have you done that before?

Just as easy as *cat* makes you think of *dog*, there are similar reactions to other words and topics.

Pencils? Related to school.

Coffee? Related to Starbucks.

Pineapple? Related to Hawaii or certain hairstyles.

Ceramics? Related to that one sexy scene in the movie *Ghost*.

SBR is a powerful conversation device because it allows you to stay in the moment and yet never run out of things to say. You won't fall into the common pitfall of trying to be present and in the moment AND trying to think about what you are going to say next. Unfortunately, most people's brains cannot do two things at once, so that is doomed to failure.

SBR lets you appear curious and engaged in the conversation, which creates the comfort necessary for rapport. You can even playfully acknowledge that you have no idea about a particular topic, and use that to seamlessly segue into something you do know about, or change the topic entirely. You will naturally be asking more questions and focusing on the other person, which tends to build balance and make the other person happy in general. That's what really matters, not the topic.

If there's a pitfall with SBR, it's focusing on one category too much. If you ask too many specific questions, you risk the conversation becoming too technical with nowhere to go. If it becomes too technical, it will become hard for you to understand and care about. The other person will likely notice your disinterest and will feel as if you are tuning them out. It creates a cycle.

And of course, if you ask too many broad questions, you can bore the other person (or yourself). This means you will be asking about the context and background— nothing substantive—and jumping from topic to topic. It feels a bit transparent. And it sounds like the kind of small talk that people love to hate.

Finally, the downside to asking too many R questions is that it makes you look as if you can't focus on anything or are perpetually distracted. It's like you keep seeing shiny objects and changing your mind based on them. It also makes it seem as if you don't care about their answers because you are immediately steering away into a different topic. This is also reminiscent of the small talk that makes networking events a nightmare for most. Avoid using this technique if you know you're liable to try and squeeze in a boast or let your ego run away with the conversation . . .

Your Patterns

Optimally, you want to be able to switch between the three categories of SBR as well as the three categories in HPM. It requires practice, and the first step is to adequately understand and master each of the six types of responses.

Once you start playing with them, patterns will start to emerge with the types of statements that come most naturally to you. We all tend to engage in specific patterns, whether we realize it or not.

Do you tend to talk more about yourself or ask questions? Are you more externally focused and present, or more in your head during conversations? Do you enjoy talk about emotions or abhor them? Do you have a bad memory that renders you useless in talking about your personal experiences?

No one can answer these questions but you. But you'll find that a few of these six response types will resonate better than the others. My pattern is a combination of History, Specific, and Related—HSR. It's just how I tend to approach and think about the world, as well as the people in it. This means I am more interested in asking questions and understand others versus sharing about myself.

Which spring most readily to *your* mind? Pick three. Maybe you're a natural talking about Philosophy, Broad and related, or you find yourself most at home with Relation and Metaphor. These are your fallback go-tos, so it might be a good place to begin. But also work on the other three, because having all of them in your pocket will make you that much better and versatile of a conversationalist. It'll save you from lopsided conversation and prevent you becoming a "one-trick pony."

The Search for Similarity and Familiarity

Think back to the last time you met someone new at a networking event or party. What was the first topic out of your mouth? It was probably one of the following:

- Where are you from?
- Who do you know here?
- How was your weekend?
- Where did you go to school?
- What do you do?

While these are normal small talk questions, we ask them instinctively not because they are great at breaking the ice. In fact, as you well know, they are usually terrible for breaking the ice and can make people feel immediately bored.

We actually ask them instinctively because we are searching for commonalities. We are searching for the "me too!" moment that can spark a deeper discussion. For instance, if we ask the question, "Where did you go to school?" we are hoping they attended the same university as us or a university where we have mutual friends. The next natural question we always ask is a variation of "Oh, wow! What a small world. Do you know James Taylor? He also went there around your time."

While you may not realize that, you are always hunting for similarities, and similarities are another way of setting a tone of friendship, familiarity, comfort, and openness. It's the type of feeling you share with your friends, and the same feeling that can instantly skyrocket your rapport.

As much as we would like to think that we are open-minded and can get along with people from every background and origin, the reality is that we usually get along best with people who we think are like us. In fact, we seek them out.

It's why places like Little Italy, Chinatown, and Koreatown exist.

But I'm not just talking about race, skin color, religion, or sexual orientation. I'm talking about people who share our values, look at the world the same way we do, and have the same take on things as we do. As the saying goes, birds of a feather flock together. This is a very common human tendency that is rooted in how our species developed. Walking out on the tundra or in a forest, you would be conditioned to avoid that which is unfamiliar or foreign because there is a high likelihood it would be interested in killing you.

Similarities make us relate better to other people because we think they'll understand us on a deeper level than other people. If we share at least one significant similarity, then all sorts of positive traits follow, because we see them as our contemporary, essentially an extension of ourselves. When you think someone is on your level, you want to connect with them because they will probably understand you better than most.

Suppose you were born in a small village in South Africa. The population of the village ranges from nine hundred to one thousand people. You now live in London and you are attending a party at a friend's home. You meet someone that also happens to be from that small village in South Africa, just eight years older so you never encountered each other.

What warm feelings will you immediately have toward this other person, and what assumptions will you make about them? How interested will you be in connecting with them and spending more time together in the future? What inside jokes or specialized points of reference can you discuss that you haven't been able to with anyone else, ever?

Hopefully that illustration drives home the value of similarity and how it drives conversational connection.

We typically use the small talk questions I mentioned at the top of this chapter to find similarity, but there are better, more effective ways to find similarities with people. For instance, we should always be *searching* for similarities or *creating* them. They both take effort and initiative.

We can *search* for similarities by asking probing questions of people and using their answers as the basis to show similarity, no matter how small. Ask questions to figure out what people are about, what they like, and how they think. Then dig deep into yourself to find small commonalities at first, such as favorite baseball teams or alcoholic drinks. Through those smaller commonalities, you'll be able to figure out what makes them tick and find deeper commonalities to instantly bond over. Just as you'd be thrilled to meet someone from that small South African town, you'd be thrilled to meet someone who shared a love of the same obscure hobby as you.

It doesn't take months or years, and it doesn't take a special circumstance like going through boot camp together. It just requires you to look outside of yourself and realize that people share common attitudes, experiences, and emotions—you just have to find them. Get comfortable asking questions and digging deeper than you naturally would. (Is it odd for you to ask five questions in a row? It shouldn't be.) It might even feel a little invasive at first. Find them and use them!

We can *create* similarities by mimicking people's body language, voice tonality, rate of speech, and overall manner of appearance. This is known as *mirroring*, and it has also been shown to produce feelings of positivity when tested (Anderson 1998). All you have to do is arrange yourself to resemble others in order to benefit from feelings of similarity, from how they are posed to how they gesture.

You can mirror their words, their tone of voice, and their mannerisms. Keep in mind that mirroring is not just about reflecting them on a wholesale basis. Instead, it is all about communicating to them that you share similar values and have the potential to connect intimately.

You can mirror physical signals, gestures, tics, and mannerisms. For example, if you notice that someone uses a lot of gestures when talking, you should do the same. Similarly, if you notice that someone's body language involves a lot of leaning and crossing of arms, you should do the same.

You can mirror their verbal expressions and expressiveness—tone of voice, inflection, word choice, slang and vocabulary, emotional intonation, and excitement and energy.
Similarities are easier to find when you share personal information and divulge details.

Statement one: You went skiing last month.

Statement two: You went skiing last month with your two brothers and you almost broke your foot.

Which of those stories is easier to relate to and find a similarity with? Obviously, the second version since there is literally three times as much information. If you are having trouble connecting with others, it's likely you are expecting to find a similarity without sharing anything yourself.

If sharing even this amount of detail feels uncomfortable and unnatural for you, it's a sign you probably don't give your conversation partners much to work with and you are essentially dropping the conversational ball when it is hit back to you. You may be the cause of awkward silence more often than not, because others will expect a back and forth flow, but they end up doing all the work while you wonder what's wrong.

In other words, get used to this feeling of discomfort because it's something you need to improve upon.

Mutual dislike is just as good as a similarity and might even be more fun. Have you noticed that it is sometimes inevitable for the conversation to remain positive, and the conversation will veer into a set of complaints about something you both dislike?

It's easy to discount these discussions because people think talking about negativity is a negative thing. However, it's absolutely valuable in your quest for connection because negativity and hate is a strong, powerful emotion.

When you check out a new restaurant, think about the reviews you'll read about it. You'll either read highly positive, gushing reviews or, more likely, the negative reviews filled with hate and spite. Hatred moves us into action like nothing else.

Some relationship counselors have even gone so far as to quip that a sign of highly successful relationships is the ability to hate the same things and people.

It's not negative to talk about negativity because it's an emotion like any other, and the more emotion you can generate in your interaction, the greater an impression you will make.

What's ultimately important is seeing eye to eye once again. How many friendships have been built in army boot camps, where the singular common bond was a hatred for the suffering they went through? How many friendships have been built on the back of hating the same teacher or morning schedule? You've bonded over common dislike far more often than you realize, so you shouldn't stray away from it.

Takeaways

- One way to be better at conversation is to learn to properly engage. We can use a six-step model for showing distressed people that we validate their experience and accept them, and these principles can be applied on a small or big scale.

- The first step in this model is simply being present, actively listening and paying attention. The second step is called accurate reflection, where you summarize and reflect what you've been told to provide further reassurance that you've understood. The third step is to gives words and labels to their emotions, which makes you seem empathetic.

- For step four, try to contextualize the person's thoughts and emotions with either recent events from their life or past experiences which might be influencing their reaction. Step five is to simply reassure the other person that their reaction is reasonable and anyone else in their position would feel the same way.

- Lastly, for step six, you can relate their experiences with your own if you've been in a similar situation. Being vulnerable can establish a stronger bond and invite further conversation and trust.

- Not all of the steps are necessary, but each of them requires us to be genuine, compassionate, receptive, and respectful—valuable skills no matter what conversation we're in.

- HPM can help with the literal content of your conversations, and stands for History (personal memories), Philosophy (opinions and thoughts), and Metaphor (what the topic reminds you of). By drawing on HPM, you'll never run out of things to say.

- Another useful acronym is SBR, which, unlike HPM which comes from within, draws inspiration from externally, and the topic itself. It stands for Specific, Broad and Related. Make a comment that drills down into the details, ask a more general question, or see what you can connect the topic at hand to, subtly changing the topic to keep the conversation flowing. You may have your own preference for each of the six and form your own unique patterns.

- When we engage with others, a golden rule of engagement is to focus on finding similarity and creating a sense of a shared experience and familiarity.

Chapter 6: Light Speed

Humor and Misdirection

Phew! Time to lighten things up, wouldn't you say? Let's turn our attention to the surprisingly versatile skills of humor or its closely related cousin, misdirection. To put it simply, misdirection is when you say one thing and then proceed with an immediate opposite. For example, "It's a secret, but let me tell you immediately," or, "That show is great, except for everyone in it." It's not rolling-in-the-aisles funny, but it definitely captures attention, and gives conversation a kind of light playfulness that most people will be happy to call wit.

It seems confusing, but what you are doing is breaking a sentence into two parts.

You're stating something in the first part, then contradicting it immediately in the second. People won't immediately be sure of what you mean, and part of the humor comes from this introduced confusion. You have both positive and negative, or vice versa, in the same sentence.

The second part of the sentence is the element that people will react to, while the first part is typically the setup. The second is your true sentiment on the topic.

This formula is the secret to the humor in such lines as George Jessel's, "The human brain is a wonderful organ. It starts to work as soon as you are born and doesn't stop until you get up to deliver a speech." Douglas Adams also used it when he said, "I love deadlines. I like the whooshing sound they make as they fly by." Here's another example: "I love dogs, but I hate seeing, hearing, and touching them," or, "This juice is awesome. Did it come from the garbage disposal?"

There's just such an appealing zing to statements like this. You can probably agree that they work, but *why* do they work?

Most of us try to be polite to people. We use euphemisms frequently, and we don't say what we really feel. The first part of a misdirecting statement is what people expect—politeness. It's you following the same old tired expected script. But then surprise! You contradict yourself and give them a dose of reality, which sets up a humorous contrast since you have deviated from what most people expect and would say themselves. As you might have observed, ironic similes also make use of misdirection to derive comedic effect. The whole effect is to send a powerful message that you don't take yourself, or the topic at hand, all that seriously. Done right, misdirection can be amazingly charming and funny—it's a way to break the rules that works so well because you appear to be using the rules at first.

Last but not least, misdirection is simply a funny way to express your feelings on something. If you really feel X about a topic, then use misdirection! "Opposite of X, but actually X," will almost always be received far better than "Gosh, I hate X."

Sarcasm is a way for people to say things without saying them, and is the most common way we use misdirection.

Think about how Chandler Bing from the television show *Friends* talks. If he says something is wonderful, he says *it's wonnnnderful* in a tone that immediately lets you know that he thinks the opposite.

Sarcasm functions like a social cue—both are ways to express something without having to explicitly say it. In that way, it's a great device for handling uncomfortable topics or pointing out the elephant in the room without directly offending people (or pointing). It allows us to walk a tightrope, as long as we don't fall into the pit of passive-aggressiveness.

At some level, most of us can appreciate sarcasm because we know what is being accomplished. It can even be the basis for your own personal brand of humor. Standup comics often use it to great effect.

Chances are, you are already using sarcasm regularly without being fully aware of it.

Sarcasm is mostly used as friendly banter with a friend or acquaintance with whom you are comfortable saying something negative. For example, consider that you've committed a minor gaffe at work, for example forgetting to return a borrowed file before it's due. If a close colleague teases you about it, you may reply with a sarcastic, "Oh yes, this is scandalous! This would for sure be in the headlines tomorrow!" But if it's your strict boss who sternly calls you out on it, you would not be likely to make a sarcastic announcement in response.

Sarcasm is usually used to poke fun at someone or something and is heavily context and audience dependent. If you are around somebody who enjoys wit and has a sarcastic sense of humor, it will be quite welcome. Sarcasm is also dynamite when used to make a playful jab at yourself—the irony is how it can have the effect of making you seem supremely confident, self-aware and intelligent. Someone might say, "Oh no, I think I've lost that twenty dollars I was holding on to . . ." and you quickly jump in with, "Oh no! What an idiot. I would never do something so thoughtless. When *I* lose money, I make sure I lose the whole wallet and everything with it."

But around others who don't share the same sense of humor, are less secure, or don't like you, it's too easy for them to interpret your attempts at sarcastic humor as a full-fledged insult. That's not what you're aiming for here. They might just think that you are an insulting jackass, or they're more inclined to listen to the first part of the misdirection than the second.

Using misdirection in the wrong context will cause people to think you lack empathy or, worse, get your jollies from hurting other people's feelings. There will be others who simply won't get the sarcasm, no matter how obvious you make it. They won't be insulted, just very confused. You'll want to avoid both outcomes. The only way to do that is to make sure you "know your audience" and start small, judge the reaction you've had, and go from there. If other people happily use sarcasm themselves, it's probably a sign that they'll appreciate yours.

Choose the correct context and sarcasm can make you more likeable and charming. It also makes you look intelligent and witty. In some social circles, appropriate levels of sarcasm are not only welcomed, but required—think of it as a refreshing antidote to humble bragging or complaining.

Now that you have a clearer idea about the proper context of sarcasm, the next step is to articulate the elements to make sure you don't just insult people left and right in your attempts at building rapport. If your annoying coworker understood sarcasm better, they might be as funny as they think they are.

For the most part, **sarcasm is saying the *opposite* of (1) an objective fact, (2) a subjective emotion, or (3) thought.**

It makes a contradictory statement about a situation to either emphasize or downplay its effect.

Objective fact: Bob plays Tetris at work constantly.

Sarcastic statement: *Bob, you are the busiest man I know.*

Subjective emotion or thought: It is hilarious that Bob plays Tetris at work constantly.

Sarcastic statement: *Bob deserves a medal for worker of the year.*

Here's another one.

Objective fact: There is a surprising amount of traffic lately.

Sarcastic statement: *What are we going to do when we get to our destination super early?*

Subjective emotion or thought: I hate traffic so much.

Sarcastic statement: *This traffic is the best part of my day.*

That's the first and most common use of sarcasm. Now let's lay out a framework for different types of sarcasm and exactly when and how you can use it. You'll be surprised how formulaic and methodical you can get with this, and subsequently with humor.

When someone says or does something very obvious, you respond by saying something equally obvious.

Bob: "That road is very long."

You: "You are very observant."

Bob: "It's so hot today!"

You: "I see you're a meteorologist in training."

Poor Bob: "This menu is huge!"

You: "Glad to see you've learned to read!"

The next application of sarcasm is when something good or bad happens. You say something about how that good or bad event reflects on the other person.

If it's good, you say that it reflects badly on them; if it's bad, you say it reflects well on them.

Bob: "I dropped my coffee mug."

You: "You've always been so graceful."

Bob: "I got an F on my math test."

You: "Now I know who to call when my calculator breaks."

You observe Poor Bob dropping a cup of coffee and state "You would make a great baseball catcher. Great hands!"

Proper delivery is crucial for sarcasm. This can mean the difference between people laughing at your sarcastic joke, or thinking that you're serious in your sentiment and branding you an overall jerk. Also keep in mind that sarcasm is perhaps the most overused technique to create humor. Use it sparingly, but effectively.

You have to make it clear that you're being sarcastic and give others a sign indicating so. Otherwise, people will feel uncomfortable at the uncertainty. Are you just being mean, or are you trying to be funny?

The most common way to do this is with a combination of a deadpan vocal tone and a wry smile or smirk. With deadpan delivery, you don't laugh while you're saying it; you appear completely serious. Then, you break into a smile to alleviate the tension and clue others in to your true intention. If paired with a genuinely nonsensical or over-the-top statement, people will put two and two together and see what you've done.

Now that you know when to deliver sarcastic remarks, it's also important to learn about how to receive them and be a good audience. Let's pretend that you are Poor Bob from earlier and insert a reply for him.

Bob: "That road is very long."

You: "You are very observant."

Bob: "You know it. I'm like an eagle."

Bob: "It's so hot today!"

You: "I see you're a meteorologist in training."

Bob: "I can feel it in my bones. It's my destiny."

Poor Bob: "This menu is huge!"

You: "Glad to see you've learned to read!"

Redeemed Bob: **"I can also count to ten."**

You need to amplify their statement and what they are implying. Does this look familiar? It's a self-deprecating remark + a witty comeback! If you can volley back a sarcastic comment without even blinking, the humor is basically guaranteed. You'll appear sharp and quick, as well as confident enough to not be flustered by an off-color remark. In fact, you signal that you're game for some witty banter, and are happy to have a bit of fun in the conversation.

When you respond to sarcasm this way, it creates a greater bond. And just as important, you don't come off as a bad sport or someone who can't take a joke. Everybody is comfortable, and you create a funny situation and potential for greater banter. This is how so many long-standing in-jokes get their start in life. If you can remember one of these witty remarks and call back to it later in the conversation, congratulations, you now have a shared conversational history with the other person—and that can be a very powerful thing.

However, there is a downside when dealing with sarcasm. A lot of people who rely on sarcastic humor, pretty much on an automatic basis, are actually masking passive-aggressive personalities. They're constantly using sarcasm as a defense mechanism to hide their true feelings. They use sarcasm to pass off their otherwise negative emotions. They might be doing this to you, so it's important to know how to sidestep their subconsciously vicious attacks.

In such cases, responding with sarcasm will only encourage them. It indicates that misusing sarcasm in that way is acceptable. If you find someone being overly sarcastic with you in ways that are passive-aggressive, approach them and politely convey that their sarcasm feels hostile, even if they didn't intend it to be so. With sarcasm, it's all about *intention*. Are you laughing *at* or *with* someone? Who is the butt of the joke, if anyone?

Next, we have irony. Irony is a type of humor that is very close to sarcasm, and often confused with it.

Here's the official definition from Dictionary.com, just because it's something that people can struggle with nailing down: "the expression of one's meaning by using language that normally signifies the opposite, typically for humorous or emphatic effect."

This is different from sarcasm in a few ways. First, irony is generally about situations and incidents, not about people. Something happens which is the opposite of what you expected. When you're presented with an irony, like a fire station burning down, it will quite obviously be ironic, and not sarcastic. However, sarcasm is usually more derogatory in nature. You're saying things you don't mean. The definition of sarcasm is "the use of irony to mock or convey contempt." Thus, you can see how saying, "You are very observant," when someone says, "This road is very long," is sarcasm, not irony, because of the element of mockery inherent in the former remark. (Naturally, you'll be using sarcasm not to insult or convey contempt, but to create humor, which will hopefully build rapport and connection.)

Ironic humor is when something that is the exact opposite of what you might expect occurs. Another way to define irony is when you say something but mean the exact opposite of what you expect.

In other words, the words that come from your mouth are the opposite of the emotion you are feeling. If you're starving, an ironic statement might be something like, "I'm so full I need to unbuckle my belt. It's like Thanksgiving in July."

Ironic humor draws its power from contrasts. There is a contrast between literal truth and perceived truth. In many cases, ironic humor stems from frustration or disappointment with our ideals. The way we imagine the world should be produces comedy when it clashes with how the world actually is.

Ironic humor is usually used to make a funny point about something or to point something out. For example, when you see a big a sign that says, "No signs allowed," that's ironic humor. The sign bans signs but is itself a sign. The expectation that the sign ensures there will be no signs in the vicinity failed.

Another example is when you see a car with a logo on the door saying, "Municipal Traffic Reduction Committee," and the car, along with everybody else, is stuck in two hours of bumper-to-bumper traffic. There is a profound ironic comedy there, as you would expect the traffic management planning committee would do a better job so they wouldn't be stuck in traffic themselves. It's like someone ordering a diet soda after they've just ordered three double cheeseburgers and fries or someone else crashing into a "thank you for not speeding" sign.

Irony is all about finding contrast and drawing some interesting and creative judgment out of it. As the examples indicate, ironic humor is more a matter of observation than one of spontaneity or creativity. You're more likely to find and point out things that are ironic than come up with something that is.

Ironic humor, on the other hand, is when you intentionally imply the opposite meaning of what you say. When we think about how to use irony conversationally, what we're really asking is what ways can we convey two messages at one time? So, your boss tells everyone to attend a meeting to discuss some issues with people being tardy to work and you slyly quip, "Sorry, Bev, is it all right if I'm ten minutes late?" with a big cheesy smile. (This, of course, depends on whether Bev is likely to find this funny or not . . .)

The Power of Improv

Let's turn our attention to a group of people who have made good banter and wit their business: improvisers and stand-up comedians.

The Rule of Improv Comedy: Great improv is a result of the creativity in spontaneous situations, and set agendas and outlines put a very low ceiling on that.

Improv comedy performances are, guess what, improvised!

The performers may occasionally work with a set theme that has been decided on beforehand, but there will always be large portions of an improv performance that involve taking direction from the crowd or audience. They can't predict what a crowd will give them to work with, so it's out of necessity that they can't have a strict agenda or outline.

That's part of the fun in attending an improv performance: you feel that you are a part of the outcome and have contributed to the show.

Obviously, these are situations where the performers have to think on their feet as quickly as possible, so they don't get tongue-tied and silent while everyone in the room is waiting. But overall, we have the perfect arena where we can watch spontaneity, curiosity, and good humor play out.

As an improv performer, you have to process what was said to you, try to project where you want the scene to go, and then predict what others might also say in response. And you have to do it all knowing that your plans might need to completely change when the other players switch things up. You have to read people's body language, try to determine if there is any ulterior message, and actively provide detail that other people can work with.

Improv comedy is collaborative in nature, but it's impossible to know what your teammates are thinking. In a split second, you need to perform a full analysis of the entire scene and spit out words that will enhance the most important aspects of it. Oh, and you're in front of a crowd of people, and there is a team of people on stage waiting on your response.

That might be the very definition of thinking on your feet (or hell on earth, if you're prone to anxiety!).

How does all of this make you a better conversationalist?

Recall that improv performances and conversations have the exact same goal—a flowing, entertaining interaction. If we look at some of the ways that improv performers are able to think fast and approach this unpredictability, we'll be able to improve our conversation skills immensely. *Without* trying too hard!

Don't Hold on Too Tightly

The first step, without a doubt, is to let go of any preconceived notion of how and where you want your conversation to go. Be "outcome independent." Professional improv players are able to create a fluid, dynamic, and witty interplay with their audience members because they are flexible and open to any possibility and direction. They are not stubborn or rigid—they understand that conversations *emerge* from the collaboration of the group and cannot be predicted or controlled too closely.

Yes, it can definitely be scary to go into a conversation with a completely blank slate, so to speak, especially if you are the type to plan and scheme. But planning and scheming has probably not gotten you too far in social conversations, so it's time to open up and let go of the talking points or agendas you want to take into your conversations with you.

Don't worry. I won't let you enter conversations unprepared—you just won't be using set agendas. By the way, when I mention set agendas, I mean goals, talking points, or objectives that people want to achieve or gain from a conversation. Your conversational resume? Sure. Your HPM and SBR tools? Absolutely. But these are temporary training wheels, and they're there to help natural conversation, not replace it.

When you talk to other people, the focus of the conversation should be about the conversation. Each conversation is its own animal, with its own inherent flow and natural rhythm. It should not be about you or what you are trying to get out of the other person or people. It shouldn't be forced to resemble a great conversation you've had before or some idea of how you think perfect conversations go. Why restrict yourself that way?

The moment other people are able to perceive your agenda, guess what happens? They will shut you out. You become somebody worthy of suspicion and skepticism. If you are trying to sell something, it makes it all that much harder once people feel that you have an ulterior motive. It's difficult to overcome the feeling that someone wants something from you. The same goes if you're trying to impress someone, to convince them of something, to get them to do this or that, to force them to pay attention to you. People want to feel like conversations are natural, fun, and something they do because they want to. Nobody wants to feel manipulated, right?

If you are approaching a conversation with an agenda, even an unconscious one, first it becomes exceedingly clear that you are only waiting for your turn to speak, and not actually listening to people. You aren't present and you aren't listening.

People might say something to you, and you might not even acknowledge their statement and just continue along with yours. You are telling them that you don't care about where the conversation is naturally heading—your agenda is more important. Others will notice your patterns sooner than you think. What are they getting out of a conversation like that?

Second, agendas leave people unready to adapt. Unless you are going to drop a speech on an audience, things will never go exactly as you plan.

When you create an agenda, you memorize it and become reliant on it. The more often that happens, the more uncomfortable we are with the unpredictability of thinking on our feet. You are essentially acting form fear—or reacting. What happens when you deviate and can't find a good place to step back into your agenda? You're left utterly unprepared for the rest of the interaction because of your reliance on what you've planned. You're no longer alive and authentic. You're like an actor on a stage who's forgotten their lines.

This is why it is extremely important to constantly listen to other people and acknowledge them. You might even go with *their* agenda. That's okay, because your goal here is to build rapport, and that will do it. Not holding on too tightly to an agenda sems scary until you realize that an agenda only gives you the illusion of control. That once you abandon it and just be in the moment, the real interesting stuff happens!

People can sometimes fall back on agendas or fixed plans out of fear or lack of confidence. They want to avoid that embarrassing moment when they're tongue-tied and awkward, unable to think of what to say next. But actually, it's those very moments that keep a conversation alive and interesting. And really, what's so wrong with finding yourself in an unexpected situation? Is it really the end of the world if you are not perfectly in control?

If you can trust yourself a little and surrender to the conversation rather than try to steer it, you give yourself opportunities to learn to become comfortable with that crucial moment, when all eyes are on you and it's time to say something. At the very least, don't underestimate the power of self-deprecating humor or a little disarming honesty:

Person A tells a witty joke, and you laugh, but suddenly feel at a loss for words and can't think of an equally funny thing to say. So, you shrug and say what you're really thinking: "You know, that's exactly the kind of brilliant joke that I could come up with, but you'll have to wait until three a.m. tomorrow morning for me to suddenly think of it..." In other words, you've made a witty joke… about not being able to make a witty joke. Congratulations, you've thought on your feet!

On the other hand, conversation is not about performance. If you can't think of anything to say, it's also a valid move to just pass the ball to someone else. Keep it going, whether all you do is ask a question, reiterate what's just happened, or use something unexpected to put the limelight back on someone else.

Learn to Make Quick Connections
Let people feel that the conversation is a two-way street. It actually becomes a two-way street when you stop, listen, and interrupt your own thoughts for theirs.

Up to this point in the chapter, we've discussed the negatives of over-preparing for conversations and coming in with outlines of what you want to discuss. Being able to rely solely on your ability to improvise is incredibly important, but just as frightening for some. So, how can we increase our capacity for quick thought?

There's no way other than through intentional practice. No, no rehearsing a script or churning out lines. But practice.

The first method is to turn on your favorite quick-witted television show with your remote in hand, because you'll be pausing constantly. For example, *30 Rock*, *Gilmore Girls*, or even *Saturday Night Live*. These are all good shows to use because there is a lot of witty banter, and direct and indirect jokes. They have the type of dialogue we want to be able to create ourselves. (Actually, for our purposes, you don't even need to watch a show you find particularly funny. It's still useful just to watch how those jokes unfold, and how energy moves between the players).

Now, pretend that you are one of the characters on the screen. It doesn't matter who you are, as long as they have a lot of interaction with other characters. Then, when other characters reply to your character on screen, pause the show and construct your own reply. Play the show again and compare your responses. What do you notice? This is going to train your ability to think through different circumstances and come up with responses.

It's not going to be easy at first. You'll probably be blank a lot of the time and not know what to say. However, if you can do this for at least fifteen minutes a day for a week, you'll eventually become quicker with your replies. It'll start to feel more comfortable, even second nature. You can also practice this exercise with podcasts and radio interviews. What you're doing is putting yourself in a position to think quickly. You can then hear what your character or avatar actually said, and you can get immediate feedback on what you could have said given the circumstances. You get to do all this at your own pace, and with the gift of being able to pause the conversation. Every piece of feedback is going to help hone your ability to come up with wit in record time.

The second method is to play free association with words and phrases. Free association is when you hear a word, then you come up with another word that the first word makes you think of. The second word can be anything, and the goal is to do this instantaneously.

For example, cat:dog, dog:puppy, puppy:paws, paws:fur, fur:allergies, allergies:medicine, medicine:nurses, nurses:doctors, doctors:plastic surgeon, plastic surgeon:fake lips, and so on. That was a free association word chain that began simply with the word cat.

How do you train this? Pick a word at random from a dictionary, and list out fifteen words in a free association word chain as quickly as possible. Then, do it again and again—verbally, because that will require the quickest thinking. The trick here is not to try too hard. Don't think about it, literally just say what pops into your head, without censorship or mulling over it.

After you grow more comfortable with random free association with words, you can take the next step and choose two random words from a dictionary and pretend they are the name of a company. Then, create a short story about what that company does, as quickly as possible.

For example, the two random words you pick are: bottle, Africa. The short story I would construct about a company named "Africa Bottle" is that they import African homemade liquors. Sure, you'll probably come up with a few doozies as you practice this, but keep your judgment at bay—your only goal is to practice being swift and relaxed making associations.

The final step of this set of free association exercises is to choose five random words from the dictionary and make up a story that involves all of the words, as quickly as possible. Let's say you choose *hiccup, elevator, heat, president,* and *fern*. Then you quickly envisage a skit where the president once got overheated in an elevator in Hawaii and thus developed hiccups, which meant he had to postpone his media conference for ten minutes while one of the aides attempted to scare him again and again behind some fern bushes in the lobby. By showing him his latest approval ratings. In a way, this is not dissimilar from what you did with the R part of SBR, or the M part of HPM.

Again, these exercises train you to think quickly and be creative, so it's imperative that you do these exercises at "full speed," so you don't have the time to step in and start second-guessing yourself. They'll be tough, and at first, your responses might be terrible. But imagine how big the difference will be between your first day and your tenth day, for example. That's the power of free association, and practice.

If you also care to analyze the similarities between free association and conversation, you might find that they are virtually the same. In conversation, you'll reply to someone on a topic, a slightly related topic, or a new topic. That's exactly the type of thought process that free association takes. In a sense, you are training yourself to come up with conversation topics quickly. In another sense, you are training yourself to trust these first impulses and not self-censor—you may be surprised, in other words, at just how creative you can be when you simply get out of your own way!

The third method is to come up with a simple structure for yourself when you're backed into a corner. For example, an easy response structure you can use for just about anything is to (1) restate what was said, (2) state an emotion, and (3) ask a question.

Here's how that looks in practice:

"So, then I punched him in the face and all was well."

"You punched him in the face? That must have been satisfying. How did it feel after?"

"Did you like the coffee?"

"Did I like the coffee? Well, I'm in a great mood now, so I guess I did. What kind was it?"

"I hear the zoos here are amazing."

"The zoos are amazing? That would make me so happy to see one. Do you want to go tomorrow?"

It's an easy template that allows you to respond to anything, even if your mind is blank, because it literally tells you what to say. So, relax; even if you're in the pickliest of pickles, getting out of it can often be as simple as that. Skip a beat and don't sweat it—you'll be witty on the next one.

Have a Little Faith

What really makes confident people feel confident? So much of the beauty in our lives is unplanned. This occurs because we are able to step outside of the boxes and limits in our heads and explore things we wouldn't have otherwise. And what results is often amazing. Confidence could be called the belief in this truth.

Over-planning and preparing is like a straitjacket for your conversation and rapport. The irony is that holding things with lightness takes far less effort than trying to force and control them, and always leads to better results. In a way, it's about committing to having better conversations rather than becoming a better conversationalist—once you get your ego out of the picture, you can actually start to let things flow. But you have to take that first step, and that takes trust.

When you remove the possibility of spontaneity from your conversations, you might feel like you are safe from spectacular failure, but you also limit the potential of how high your conversation can soar. In other words, it's safe but boring.

The most memorable moments do not typically come because somebody planned them that way. In fact, it's usually the opposite.

Here's a quick thought experiment that will bolster your sense of confidence in the face of unpredictability. Hopefully it will help you realize that you don't need an agenda, and that your worst-case scenario is not really that bad.

Pick five topics that you know absolutely nothing about. Bring them up one by one with a friend. Commit to talking about each topic for at least five minutes. See the various angles and routes you can go to make a topic interesting. Grasp for straws on how to keep a dialogue going. Notably, see how you can relate it to other topics, and see how easy it is to get side-tracked onto something else. There's not much to fear, is there? You might convince yourself of something interesting: that the content of a conversation is only secondary, and your attitude and energy play a much, much bigger role.

The 1:1:1 Method of Storytelling

On the theme of simplifying storytelling, we've been talking about how we can use a mini story in many ways. You may be wondering what the difference is between a *mini* story and a *full-fledged* story.

To me, not much. As I mentioned, many people like to complicate storytelling as if they were composing an impromptu Greek tragedy. Does there have to be an introduction, middle, struggle, then resolution? You may have read that great stories are about X, Y, and Z; that you need a beginning, middle, and ending; that you should use as much descriptive detail as possible; or how important pauses are. That's one way of doing it, but certainly not the easiest or most practical.

My method of storytelling in conversation is to prioritize the discussion afterward— similar to what you saw with the fallback stories in an earlier chapter. This means that the story itself doesn't need to be that in-depth or long. It can and should contain specific details that people can relate to and latch on to, but it doesn't need to have parts or stages. It can be *mini* by nature. That's why it's called the *1:1:1 method*.

It stands for a story that (1) has one action, (2) can be summed up in one sentence, and (3) evokes one primary emotion in the listener. You can see why they're short and snappy. They also tend to make sure that you know your point before starting and have a very low chance of verbally wandering for minutes and alienating your listeners.

For a story to consist of *one action* means only one thing is happening. The story is about one occurrence. It should be direct and straightforward. Anything else just confuses the point and makes you liable to ramble.

A story should be able to be *summed up* in one sentence because, otherwise, you are trying to convey too much. This step actually takes practice, because you are forced to think about which aspects matter and which don't add anything to your action. It's a skill to be able to distill your thoughts into one sentence and still be thorough—often, you won't realize what you want to say unless you can do this.

Finally, a story should focus on one primary emotion to be evoked in the listener. And you should be able to name it! Keep in mind that evoking an emotion ensures that your story actually has a point, and it will color what details you carefully choose to emphasize that emotion. For our purposes here, there really aren't that many emotions you might want to evoke in others from a story. You might have humor, shock, awe, envy, happiness, anger, or annoyance. Those are the majority of reasons we relate our experiences to others.

Keep in mind that it's just my method for conveying my experiences to others. Whether people hear two sentences about a dog attack or they hear ten sentences doesn't change the impact of the story. The reason I abbreviate stories is so the conversation can move forward and we can then focus on the listener's impact and reaction. So what does this so-called story sound like?

"I was attacked by a dog and I was so frightened I nearly wet my pants." It's one

sentence, there is one action, and the bit about wetting the pants is to emphasize the fact that the emotion you want to convey is fear and shock.

You could include more detail about the dog and the circumstances, but chances are people are going to ask about that immediately, so let them guide what they want to hear about your story. Invite them to participate! Very few people want to sit and listen to a monologue, most of which is told poorly and in a scattered manner. Therefore, keep the essentials but cut your story short, and let the conversation continue as a shared experience rather than you monopolizing the airspace. Make it a shared experience rather than all about you.

The 1:1:1 method can be summed up as starting a story as close to the end as possible. Most stories end before they get to the end, in terms of impact on the listener, their attention span, and the energy that you have to tell it. In other words, many stories tend to drone on because people try to adhere to these rules or because they simply lose the plot and are trying to find it again through talking. Above all else, a long preamble is not necessary. What's important is that people pay attention, care, and will react in some (preferably) emotional manner.

Ask for Stories

Most of the focus with stories is usually on telling them—but what about soliciting them from others and allowing them to feel as good as you do when a story lands well? What about stepping aside and giving other people the spotlight? Well, it's just a matter of how you ask for them.

When you watch sports, one of the most illogical parts is the post-game or post-match interview. These athletes are still caught in the throes of adrenaline, out of breath, and occasionally drip sweat on to the reporters.

Yet when you are watching a broadcaster interview an athlete, does anything odd strike you about the questions they ask? The interviewers are put into an impossible situation and usually walk away with decent soundbites—at the very least, not audio disasters. Their duty is to elicit a coherent answer from someone who is mentally incoherent at the moment. How do they do that?

They'll ask questions like: "So tell me about that moment in the second quarter. What did you feel about it and how did the coach turn it around then?" as opposed to: "How'd you guys win?" or: "How did you turn this match around, come back, and pull out all the stops to grab the victory at the very end?" as opposed to: "How was the comeback?"

The key? They ask for a story rather than an answer. They phrase their inquiry in a way that can only be answered with a story, in fact.

Detail, context, and boundaries are given for the athletes to set them up to talk as much as possible instead of providing a breathless one-word answer. It's almost as if they provide the athletes with an outline of what they want to hear and how they can proceed. They make it easy for them to tell a story and simply engage. It's like if someone asks you a question but, in the question, tells you exactly what they want to hear as hints.

Sometimes we think we are doing the heavy lifting in a conversation and the other party isn't giving us much to work with. But that's a massive cop-out. They might not be giving you much, but you also might be asking them the wrong questions, which is making them give you terrible responses. In fact, if you think you are shouldering the burden, you are definitely asking the wrong questions.

Conversation can be much more pleasant for everyone involved if you provide fertile ground for people to work in. Don't set the other person up to fail and be a poor conversationalist; that will only make you invest and care less and cause the conversation to die out.

When people ask me low-effort, vague questions, I know they probably aren't interested in the answer. They're just filling the time and silence. To create win-win conversations and better circumstances for all, ask for stories the way the sports broadcasters do. Ask questions in a way that makes people want to share.

Stories are personal, emotional, and compelling. There is a thought process and narrative that necessarily exists. They are what show your personality and are how you can learn about someone. They show people's emotions and how they think. Last but not least, they show what you care about.

Compare this with simply asking for closed-ended answers. Answers are often too boring and routine for people to care. They will still answer your questions but in a very literal way, and the level of engagement won't be there. Peppering people with shallow questions puts people in a position to fail conversationally.

It's the difference between asking, "What was the best part of your day so far? Tell me how you got that parking space so close!" instead of just, "How are you?"

When you ask somebody the second question, you're asking for a quick, uninvolved answer. You're being lazy and either don't care about their answer or want them to carry the conversational burden. When you ask somebody one of the first two questions, you're inviting them to tell a specific story about their day. You are inviting them to narrate the series of events that made their day great or not. And it can't really be answered with a one-word answer.

Another example is "What is the most exciting part of your job? How does it feel to make a difference like that?" instead of simply asking them the generic "What do you do?" When you only ask somebody what they do for a living, you know exactly how the rest of the conversation will go: "Oh, I do X. What about you?"

A final example is: "How did you feel about your weekend? What was the best part? It was so nice outside," instead of just: "How was your weekend?"

Prompting others for stories instead of simple answers gives them a chance to speak in such a way that they feel emotionally invested. This increases the sense of meaning they get from the conversation you're having with them. It also makes them feel you are genuinely interested in hearing their answer because your question doesn't sound generic.

Consider the following guidelines when asking a question:

1. Ask for a story
2. Be broad but with specific directions or prompts
3. Ask about feelings and emotions
4. Give the other person a direction to expand their answer into, and give them multiple prompts, hints, and possibilities
5. If all else fails, directly ask "Tell me the story about . . ."

Imagine that you want the other person to inform your curiosity. Other examples include the following:

1. "Tell me about the time you . . ." versus "How was that?"
2. "Did you like that . . ." versus "How was it?"
3. "You look focused. What happened in your morning . . ." versus "How are you?"

Let's think about what happens when you elicit (and provide) personal stories instead of the old, tired automatic replies.

You say hello to your co-worker on Monday morning and you ask how his weekend was. At this point, you have cataloged what you will say in case he asks you the same. Remember, they probably don't care about the actual answer ("good" or "okay"), but they *would* like to hear something interesting. But you never get the chance, because you ask him "How was your weekend? Tell me about the most interesting part—I know you didn't just watch a movie at home!"

He opens up and begins to tell you about his Saturday night when he separately and involuntarily visited a strip joint, a funeral, and a child's birthday party. That's a conversation that can take off and get interesting, and you've successfully bypassed the unnecessary and boring small talk that plagues so many of us.

Most people love talking about themselves. Use this fact to your advantage. Once someone takes your cue and starts sharing a story, make sure you are aware of how you're responding to that person through your facial expressions, gestures, body language, and other nonverbal signals. Since there is always at least one exciting thing in any story, focus on that exciting point and don't be afraid to show that you're engaged.

One quick tip to show that you're engaged and even willing to add is something I call *pinning the tail on the donkey*. There is probably a better name for it, but my vocabulary was severely lacking at the time. The donkey is the story from someone else, while the tail is your addition to it. It allows you to feel like you're contributing, it makes other people know you're listening, and it turns into something you've created together.

People will actually love you for it because, when you do this, your mindset becomes focused on assisting people's stories and letting them have the floor.

Bob's story: "I went to the bank and tripped and spilled all my cash, making it rain inadvertently."

Tail: **"Did you think you were Scrooge McDuck for a second?"**

When you make a tail, try to home in on the primary emotion the story was conveying, then add a comment that amplifies it. The story was about how Bob felt rich, and Scrooge McDuck is a duck who swims in pools of gold doubloons, so it adds to the story and doesn't steal Bob's thunder. Get into the habit of assisting other people's stories. It's easy, witty, and extremely likable because you are helping them out.

Conversational diversity
Hypotheticals
A hypothetical is a classic conversational diversification tactic. Okay, that's a fancy term for what really amounts to, "Hey, what would you do if . . ." and "What do you think about . . ."

But here's what happens when you throw a hypothetical into your conversation. You inject exponentially the amount of variability and unpredictability possible because it's likely something your conversation partner has never considered, and the hypothetical you pose will be something that has no clear or correct answer. Instead, something hopefully exciting comes out of it and you get to discuss something that would never have come up otherwise.

Use hypotheticals to see how people react and how their minds work. You'll learn something about them from how they answer, and you can treat the hypothetical itself like an inkblot test—how they answer probably says something about them. In the end, wherever it goes will probably be more interesting than an interview!

The easiest way to make a conversation awkward or to introduce dead space is to ask questions that can easily be answered by a simple yes or no. Open-ended questions allow for creativity. They allow people to dig into their memory banks, come up with random associations, or otherwise trigger their imagination. With that said, your hypothetical question should be challenging enough so that the recipient actually needs to be a bit creative in answering the question.

The secret to hypotheticals is to make them appear spontaneous. Ask for their opinion on something out of curiosity. You don't want to come off as contrived or like you're reading from a script. That's going to make you look ingenuous. And you don't want to seem as if you have some sort of agenda.

Adding a one- to two-sentence backstory as to why this thought "spontaneously" popped into your mind tends to help.

Finally, keep in mind that when you use these, you must also have an answer prepared for the hypothetical you ask. You can step in with your answer while they are formulating theirs—and you should have thought about this answer beforehand so you can be prepared and rehearse it. Don't be in a situation where you don't know the answer to your own hypothetical. You don't need a definitive answer, but you at least need a stance or opinion. There's nothing worse than your conversation partner saying, "I don't know," and you also saying, "I don't know." Nothing else will fill that space besides awkward silence.

Here are some examples of hypothetical questions you can toss into your conversations like a grenade. It's a good rule of thumb to have a few prepared and up your sleeve for when you sense you are falling into some type of routine or pattern.

Type #1: What would you do if . . .

Example: What would you do if the waiter from lunch screamed at you to give him a bigger tip?

Type #2: Would you rather have this or that?

Example: Would you rather be four inches shorter or sixteen inches taller?

Type #3: My friend just did/said this . . . What would you have done?

Example: My friend just called out his boss for working too much. Can you imagine that? What would you have done?

Type #4: What if you were in this situation . . .?

Example: What if your co-worker was stealing your food from the fridge every day? How would you handle that?

Type #5: Which of the following . . .?

Example: Which do you think is better: super cold winters or hot summers?

Type #6: Who do you think . . .?

Example: Which of us do you think got the best grades in school? Or the worst?

Think Out Loud

This is a rather simplistic way of phrasing it, but thinking out loud can introduce quite a bit of conversational diversity. We filter ourselves far too much, and while it's called for sometimes, it doesn't always help.

If we just voice our inner monologue about what we're thinking about during our day, this can be quite an icebreaker. Share your thoughts about your surroundings or what you observe around you. Share what you are doing, what you are seeing, what you are thinking, and what you are wondering. Thinking out loud can also just be voicing your feelings, such as, "I'm so happy with the sunshine right now," or, "I can't believe the coffee here is so expensive!"

This will lead to a more open flow of communication. Others will feel less guarded around you and that can lead to a higher level a mutual comfort. It's also bound to be more interesting than filling the silence with a question that no one cares about.

Just say what's on your mind and you are inviting others to speak, but it's not a demand.

The added benefit is you'll probably end up being that person who says what everyone is thinking but is afraid to say. Maybe they're just shy or want to seem polite.

Whatever it is, they are thinking it, but they feel it's not proper to voice their thoughts aloud. If you become that person who is the first to say what everyone is thinking, you break the ice.

People will feel they can trust you and be comfortable around you because you actually have the guts to say what they wanted to say. At least you'll bring up some common ground that others can comment on.

Takeaways

- Lightness, humor and playfulness are the life blood of good conversation, and there are ways to develop them for yourself.
- One quick technique is misdirection, where a statement has two parts: the first is expected and ordinary, the second contradicts it with unexpected and comedic results. Sarcasm can be powerful but is best when directed at yourself and used with those you are more familiar with. Ironic humor is similar to sarcasm, but more focused on

the observation of the contrast between the expected and the actual.

- The world of improv has a lot to teach us about good conversational chemistry. One improv rule is not to hold on to any outcome too tightly, and be ready to follow the emerging flow of the conversation.
- Another rule is to rely on quick connections to make sure you always have something to say. This can be practiced by free associating one, two, or five words. Good improv is about having faith in the conversation's direction, and your ability to be okay with where it goes.
- The 1:1:1 method of storytelling is a mini story technique that relies on one action, summarized in one sentence, that evokes one main emotion in the listener. This keeps your stories engaging, short, and effective. Alternatively, you can ask for other people's stories.
- Conversational diversity is about having as many different tools in your toolkit as possible. Hypothetical questions are one such tool. These kinds of "what if . . .?" questions inject some excitement, creativity, and unpredictability, while

showing something interesting about the person giving the answer.

- Finally, thinking out loud can be a way to turn monologues into dialogues. If we speak freely and without self-censoring, we break the ice, share ourselves honestly, and invite (rather than demand) others to join us.

Summary Guide

CHAPTER 1. CONVERSATIONAL LANDMINES

- Small talk is not a mysterious inbuilt trait but a skill anyone can learn and master. Being better at conversation is about understanding the real goal of any small talk: to foster closer and more genuine human connections with others.
- There are many barriers to this connection, and these are habits and mindsets to avoid. If we treat the goal of conversation as a way to play at being an ideal version of ourselves (the cool guy), we risk coming across as fake, desperate, or unlikable.
- If we see the goal of conversation as a chance to prove how right or how intelligent we are, we miss an opportunity to genuinely learn about the other person and enjoy one of the main perks of dialogue: delving into someone else's perspective.

- If we see the goal of conversation as a battle or context to win, or a way to demonstrate our superiority, we treat our conversation partners like enemies or merely an audience, and this definitely stops the natural flow of conversation and prevents bonding.
- If we see the goal of conversation as a way to prove our value as human beings, we may be tempted to brag and boast. But this has the opposite effect and make us unlikable—plus, humble bragging is nearly always very transparent!
- Finally, a big barrier to genuine connection and rapport is simply not being on the same wavelength, or mismatched energies. We can learn to be better at this by matching our posture, what we're saying, and how we speak to the person we're talking to.

CHAPTER 2. GET YOURSELF RIGHT

- To be a better conversationalist and a small talk natural, it makes sense to prepare. Before you even have a conversation, make sure that you're in the right mindset. This may take practice.

- Use "barista practice" to help you get warmed up and into the socializing mindset. We naturally assume we will dislike connecting with others, when research shows the opposite. But we can get rusty! Barista practice is finding ways to have one- to ten-second-long mini-interactions with waiters, cashiers and service staff to get yourself in the small talk habit.

- Reading out loud is an exercise that can help you physically warm your vocal cords and get you feeling comfortable in your own voice. Read a chosen passage out loud with as much variability in emotion, tone, pitch, accent, pace, and volume to stretch your expressive powers and get you feeling confident and warmed up.

- Another way to boost confidence as you're learning to improve small talk skills is to fashion a role model that you then emulate. Ask what they would do in any socially tense situation, and what exact traits they have that you admire. The psychological distance and sense of safety can be just what you need to bootstrap those traits in yourself.

- Many of us feel like we are boring and don't have anything interesting to say, or we freeze when asked questions. A great approach is to think in terms of telling mini stories to engage interest and capture the emotional investment of your audience.

- Prepare beforehand by thinking of a few potential mini stories to share when prompted with questions—a few sentences are enough. This can be thought of as a conversational résumé and will help you avoid awkward silences or freezing and not knowing what to say.

CHAPTER 3. SET THE MOOD

- Connection with others is a wonderful thing, but how do we set the mood? We need to create the conditions to make good conversational chemistry flow. One big way is to divulge information about ourselves voluntarily, to get the conversation moving along.

- Oversharing may seem like something to avoid, but there is plenty of research to suggest that honestly opening up to others actually makes them like and trust us more. You'll distinguish yourself from the automatic stereotypes by giving specific details about yourself, and make your life seem more interesting and compelling.
  - We can divulge both by revealing additional information or by confessing to how we feel, sharing a story or revealing something unexpected about ourselves. People bond over emotional identification, so don't worry about appearing weak or vulnerable—divulging will actually encourage others to do the same and foster good rapport.
  - When you're asked a question, try responding with three or four pieces of information. Try sharing mini stories about your experiences, your memories, your hopes and dreams.
  - Oversharing is almost always a good idea, except if you are hogging the conversation to do it!
  - Self-amusement and self-entertainment are not a technique

but a mindset, and a shift from focusing on what you ought to do for others, onto your own experience in the conversation.

- We can develop this attitude in ourselves by staying curious and open-ended, thinking of conversations as play, refusing to self-censor or second guess ourselves, being a little more assertive and brave in our self-disclosure, and being genuine and spontaneous rather than relying on old stuffy rules.

- With self-amusement, we come across as more relaxed, confident, and attractive to others. We are no longer desperately trying to win approval or attaching to any outcome, but experimenting to see what happens, and where the conversation goes. This flexible spirit is precisely what makes a conversation really "click."

CHAPTER 4. INTERACT AND PARTICIPATE FULLY

- In order to interact and engage more fully in conversations, we need to work against our not-so-useful habits and learn better ones.
- A non-negotiable habit is becoming a master at using questions. The right questions help people feel closer to us, communicate our attention and care, share our competence, show that we're aware and paying attention, deepen intimacy, guide the conversation, and make us more trustworthy.
- All exchanges, and hence all questions, are typically on one of three possible levels: those exchanging factual information, those exchanging feelings and emotions, and those communicating deeper values. In social situations, you'll lean more heavily on the last two, but a good conversation works when people have similar conversational goals and are matched in the level they're interacting on.
- Conversational narcissism is an impediment to curiosity, engagement, and good question asking. Whether unconscious or conscious, this usually results from us placing something other than connection with the other person

263

as our goal for conversation, i.e. to brag, to defend, to compete.

- We can reduce our own conversational narcissism by using questions. Follow-up questions are very effective, as are open-ended questions that don't make people uncomfortable, but may *gently* push on the barrier or normal etiquette.

- Just as a role model can be a guide and inspiration for your own behavior, a model can also help you stay curious when you talk to others. Talk show hosts are experts and placing their conversation partners front and center, so we can ask, what would they do? Usually, the answer is "treat my guest like the most interesting person in the whole universe."

- Curiosity needs to be genuine. We all have a bias against others sometimes, assuming they're not very interesting, but unless we ask, we won't learn about their more fascinating sides. Assume that everyone has something to teach you, and foster a genuine inquisitiveness into the details of their world. I guarantee you will not be disappointed.

CHAPTER 5. ENGAGEMENT

- One way to be better at conversation is to learn to properly engage. We can use a six-step model for showing distressed people that we validate their experience and accept them, and these principles can be applied on a small or big scale.

- The first step in this model is simply being present, actively listening and paying attention. The second step is called accurate reflection, where you summarize and reflect what you've been told to provide further reassurance that you've understood. The third step is to gives words and labels to their emotions, which makes you seem empathetic.

- For step four, try to contextualize the person's thoughts and emotions with either recent events from their life or past experiences which might be influencing their reaction. Step five is to simply reassure the other person that their reaction is reasonable and anyone else in their position would feel the same way.

- Lastly, for step six, you can relate their experiences with your own if you've been in a similar situation. Being vulnerable can establish a stronger bond and invite further conversation and trust.

- Not all of the steps are necessary, but each of them requires us to be genuine, compassionate, receptive, and respectful—valuable skills no matter what conversation we're in.

- HPM can help with the literal content of your conversations, and stands for History (personal memories), Philosophy (opinions and thoughts), and Metaphor (what the topic reminds you of). By drawing on HPM, you'll never run out of things to say.

- Another useful acronym is SBR, which, unlike HPM which comes from within, draws inspiration from externally, and the topic itself. It stands for Specific, Broad and Related. Make a comment that drills down into the details, ask a more general question, or see what you can connect the topic at hand to, subtly changing the topic to keep the conversation flowing. You may have your own preference for each of the six and form your own unique patterns.

- When we engage with others, a golden rule of engagement is to focus on finding similarity and creating a sense of a shared experience and familiarity.

CHAPTER 6: LIGHT SPEED

- Lightness, humor and playfulness are the life blood of good conversation, and there are ways to develop them for yourself.
- One quick technique is misdirection, where a statement has two parts: the first is expected and ordinary, the second contradicts it with unexpected and comedic results. Sarcasm can be powerful but is best when directed at yourself and used with those you are more familiar with. Ironic humor is similar to sarcasm, but more focused on the observation of the contrast between the expected and the actual.
- The world of improv has a lot to teach us about good conversational chemistry. One improv rule is not to hold on to any

outcome too tightly, and be ready to follow the emerging flow of the conversation.

- Another rule is to rely on quick connections to make sure you always have something to say. This can be practiced by free associating one, two, or five words. Good improv is about having faith in the conversation's direction, and your ability to be okay with where it goes.
- The 1:1:1 method of storytelling is a mini story technique that relies on one action, summarized in one sentence, that evokes one main emotion in the listener. This keeps your stories engaging, short, and effective. Alternatively, you can ask for other people's stories.
- Conversational diversity is about having as many different tools in your toolkit as possible. Hypothetical questions are one such tool. These kinds of "what if . . .?" questions inject some excitement, creativity, and unpredictability, while showing something interesting about the person giving the answer.
- Finally, thinking out loud can be a way to turn monologues into dialogues. If we speak freely and without self-censoring,

we break the ice, share ourselves honestly, and invite (rather than demand) others to join us.

56177588R00150